A CONSCIOUS LEADERSHIP COLLECTIVE

LEADING
FROM WITHIN

CEASING AND DESISTING THE INTERNAL B.S.

AN ANTHOLOGY PRESENTED BY:

CHANTÉE L. CHRISTIAN

FOREWORD BY: ANGELA R. MCCULLOUGH

A CONSCIOUS LEADERSHIP COLLECTIVE

LEADING FROM WITHIN

CEASING AND DESISTING THE INTERNAL B.S.

AN ANTHOLOGY PRESENTED BY:

CHANTÉE L. CHRISTIAN

FOREWORD BY: **ANGELA R. MCCULLOUGH**

CONSCIOUS AUTHORS

JACQUELYN BSHARAH, PHD | DIONNE GALLOWAY | DARCI L. GRAVES

JAMES T. HARRIS | DOMINIQUE HOLLINS | DYANA LANGLEY-ROBINSON

MARQUISE "BOGEY" MCCOY | MINETTA MINOR | CARL MOSBY III

JENNIFER PIHLAJA | ASHLEY B. STEWART

 CCMEDIA

Published in the United States by: CC Media, LLC (a subsidiary of My Best SHIFT, LLC)
www.ccmediaproductions.net, www.mybestshift.com,
Arlington, Virginia 22206

Cover design by MaeArt Creative
Cover photography by Life of a Fat Kid, LLC
Interior design by CC Media, LLC and MaeArt Creative

eBook ISBN: 979-8-9995433-1-8
Paperback ISBN: 979-8-9995433-0-1
B&N Paperback ISBN: 979-8-9995433-6-3
Hardcover ISBN: 979-8-9995433-2-5

First Edition: October 2025

PRAISE FOR
LEADING FROM WITHIN

"All leadership is, first and foremost, self-leadership. In a time when many seem to want to be leaders but few truly lead, *Leading From Within* is an invitation to become the positive change we must now create. What's at stake is our future—our now. This book is -most definitely one of them."

—Elisabet Lahti, PhD
Founder of Sisu Lab | Author of *Gentle Power*

"At Emerge, the nation's largest network of women elected officials and candidates, we train women on how to lead with purpose, integrity, and authenticity. This is the type of leadership we need in these times. That's why this book resonated so strongly with me. It not only touches on these themes, it is a model for how to do this in the world."

—A'shanti F. Gholar
President & CEO, Emerge

"*Leading From Within* is a thought-provoking and inclusive view of leader development through a series of very personal experiences. These experiences bring the internal leadership journey alive and prompt an interior view of our own conscious growth as leaders."

—Lori Mazan
Co-Founder, Sounding Board, Inc. |
Author of *Leadership Revolution*

"Leadership doesn't begin with your title—it begins with your inner work and your commitment to first leading yourself. The Conscious Leadership Collective is a reminder that when we do the inner work with confidence, courage, and authenticity, we unlock an impactful leadership that transforms not only ourselves but those we lead. This book is more than inspiration—it's a blueprint for attaining true leadership."

—Ashlye V. Wilkerson, PhD
Dynamic Speaker, Leadership Expert, Motivator | Author |
University Trustee | Host & Thought Leader for Phenomenal
Women Leading

ALSO BY CC MEDIA, LLC

(a subsidiary of My Best SHIFT, LLC)

Awareness Put Me On: Leading By Choice, Thriving By Design

12 Shades of Empowerment: Monthly Affirmations for Black

Women (Coloring Book)

You're Dope AF (52 Affirmations)

You could be anywhere in the world, yet you chose to be here, with us. For that, we are deeply grateful.

This book is for anyone who has ever felt unseen, unheard, misunderstood, or unworthy. May these pages remind you that you are enough, your story matters, and your lived experience is real and valid.

Leading From Within is a radical act of healing, becoming, and choosing to lead from truth, not theory. It's for those breaking cycles, building legacies, and daring to believe that dreams do come true.

We see you. Keep moving.

We are you. Keep steady.

We are in this together.

We got this!

Leading From Within

TABLE OF CONTENTS

SETTING THE STAGE

PART I
TURNING INWARD – THE QUIET WORK OF HEALING

"You don't heal by moving on. You heal by moving in—into the pain, the lessons, the truth of who you are." -Unknown

PART II
ALIGNMENT & PURPOSE

"Don't ask what the world needs. Ask what makes you come alive, and go do it. Because what the world needs is people who have come alive." — Howard Thurman

PART III
AUTHENTIC LEADERSHIP IN ACTION

"Authenticity is the daily practice of letting go of who we think we're supposed to be and embracing who we are." — Brené Brown

PART IV
SYSTEMS, LEGACY & COLLECTIVE CONSCIOUSNESS

"We are ancestors in training. The choices we make today write the stories future generations will inherit." — Unknown

CCMEDIA

FOREWORD
ANGELA R. MCCULLOUGH

E verything you think you know about leadership is a lie. Leadership is not about being the loudest, having a title, or occupying the corner office. Leadership is something deeper.

Leadership is about how you see, serve, and stand with people.

It is also about you. The quiet moment when you walk in integrity. When you decide it matters more to lead as you are than how society says you should.

I learned this in rooms where the pressure to conform was suffocating and the stakes were high. What saved me was not status; I had no option left. I had to choose myself.

Leadership stakes are higher than ever. Leaders are unraveling, and so is the world. Too many conform, saying or doing only what seems safe.

We lack leaders who stand in truth, speak their story, and lift others. When leadership fails, it fails the people and the mission.

My reckoning came after more than thirty years in the aviation industry. I served as the Acting Deputy Chief Operating Officer responsible for the National Airspace System. Thirty thousand people. An eleven-billion-dollar budget. On paper, it was the dream job. The pinnacle.

In reality, I was misaligned. The work was relentless, the spotlight constant, and expectations everywhere, even unspoken. On the surface it looked like success, but inside I was suffocating.

Choosing not to seek the role permanently was the hardest decision of my career. I did not doubt my ability. I knew the position no longer aligned with my values. That choice forced me to face what leadership meant to me.

I stopped measuring leadership by size and scale. I started asking if I was in alignment with myself. Walking away was harder than I expected because the world said it should have been my defining moment.

Authentic leadership is pivoting when your values and role no longer align.

Stepping away from the role was my reclamation.

The authors in this book know that truth oh too well. Conscious leadership begins when you turn inward before turning outward. It calls you to face your patterns. To speak your truth. To act from your deepest values.

The stories in this book don't offer polish. They offer honesty. Leaders here move through disruption, grief, illness, and betrayal. They rebuild by standing in who they are, not in what others expected. They show us that vulnerability has weight, boundaries matter, and sometimes walking away is the strongest move.

What makes these voices powerful is their refusal to edit out the truth. They speak about depression, cancer, racism, burnout, and unraveling with the same candor they bring to joy, healing, and renewal. In doing so, they dismantle the myth that leaders must be untouchable, and they reveal something far more powerful: leaders who are whole.

This is what leadership demands now. No shortcuts. No easy fixes. We need people willing to do the slow work of inner change. Leaders who know that healing themselves is service. Leaders who can sit in complexity and still guide others toward clarity.

The leadership crisis is characterized by a lack of congruence, where leaders say one thing but do another. The future belongs to those who truly live their values.

As you read, you will encounter voices that are raw and deeply human. They will challenge you. They will steady you and remind you that leadership is not about having all the answers. True leadership is about living honestly, walking in clarity, and consciously leaving room for others to rise alongside you.

And here's your invitation. Don't just read the stories, actively reflect on and engage with them. Explore how they challenge or affirm your definition of leadership. Be courageous and lead from your truth. As you do, remember this: your light, your voice, and your presence are not only enough. They are urgently needed. Step into them now and watch what shifts.

INTRODUCTION
CHANTÉE L. CHRISTIAN

"This anthology is our response to a world hungry for a new narrative of leadership, one that redefines success, honors presence, embraces awareness, accepts authenticity, and centers integrity. Leading From Within is a mirror reflecting what's possible when leaders choose to go inward before leading outward."

— *Chantée L. Christian*

If you've been moving so fast that your reflection feels a little unfamiliar, pause.

You are in the right place.

Welcome to a collective exploration into the power of (re)defining leadership. *A Conscious Leadership Collective*, Volume I: *Leading From Within* is a bold literary movement and the natural next step in a much-needed leadership evolution.

This anthology was born from the energy of the 2025 *Conscious Leadership Summit* (CLS). Unlike the typical professional experience, CLS was a curated gathering designed to reignite passion, fuel growth, and build a vibrant community of leaders who lead with intention and integrity. It was inspired by the bestselling authors of *Awareness Put Me On*, and rooted in the belief that leadership must be (re)imagined, (re)examined,
(re)evaluated, and (re)defined. In other words: Leading. Consciously.

Leading From Within is Volume I of a six-part series exploring the full arc of conscious leadership. This series doesn't just explore ideas—it elevates lived experience. It centers presence over performance, depth over decorum, and purpose over pretense. It is leadership (re)claimed, (re)imagined, and rooted in humanity.

Full disclaimer: This book is a curation of real stories from real leaders. Truth-tellers, disruptors, and change agents who are redefining what leadership looks and feels like when it's led from within. It is not designed to be a full-on playbook. It is meant to be a mirror. I am an avid believer that you don't attract what you want; you attract who you are. And through that lens, certain chapters and authors will feel like they're speaking directly to you because in many ways, they are.

(RE)INTRODUCTION
Before we get too far into the introduction of this powerful body of work, allow me to (re)introduce myself. I'm Chantée L. Christian, your official *Ambassador of Awareness* on this expedition. The cultural nods sprinkled throughout this introduction and my chapter are very intentional. You're welcome! Consider them a gift from me to you.

Who am I? I am a catalyst for growth, change, and inspired action. Through my own evolution, I've embraced the call to walk beside others as they uncover their voice, expand their impact, and lead with purpose. I'm honored to be a curator of spaces and stories that amplify voices, challenge norms, and shift the narrative of what was.

As the founder of CC Media, LLC, the award-winning multimedia imprint behind the My Best SHIFT podcast, the Unspoken Truths series, and the international bestseller *Awareness Put Me On*, I've had the privilege of cultivating stories that move hearts, shift minds, and create rippling effects far beyond my wildest dreams. I expect nothing less from Leading From Within.

Together, we are setting the tone for what's next.

Transformation over tradition. Awareness over autopilot. Intention in every step.

LEADING FROM THE INSIDE OUT

As your *Ambassador of Awareness* on this reflective and introspective journey, I invite you to pause and consider: Who are you when no one's watching? More importantly, what conscious (or unconscious) place are you leading from? Remember, whether it's personal or professional, who you are in one space is who you are in all spaces. It may manifest or look different depending on the environment, but the result is the same.

Buckle up, friend! You are about to embark on a transformative adventure, one that begins with that opening question. As you dive into the pages of *Leading From Within*, I invite you to not just think about them intellectually. Sit with them from a space of deep introspective, rooted in bravery, and alive with a wild courageous energy that stirs something up in your soul. This isn't just about reflection. It is, however, about reclamation—of self, of truth, of the power you've always held.

This anthology is a space for truth-telling, for authenticity at its core. A place to honor the messy, magical process of becoming. Curated by a diverse collective of leaders, each consciously redefining what it means to lead in today's world, *Leading From Within* weaves lived experience, personal transformation, and wisdom shaped by trial and error to challenge outdated models of performance-based leadership.

Through deeply personal essays, each author shares their journey of leading with vulnerability, authenticity, and radical self-awareness— offering you a mirror, a map, and a moment of reckoning. Because leadership is more than performance. It's presence. It's alignment. AND this redefined version of leadership is an open invitation for you to return to who you've always been—before the titles, before the expectations, before the noise and the weight of the world.

We have intentionally cultivated a space where leaders felt brave enough to go beyond the surface—the same surface-level narratives that have cluttered bookshelves for far too long (no shade...*Okay*, maybe just a little). These authors dug deep so you could feel seen, heard, inspired, and reminded that you are not alone. Brené Brown reminds us, "You can't get to courage without rumbling with vulnerability." Let me assure you, the courage shown in these pages is unmatched. Naval Ravikant said, "To write a great book, you must first become the book."

These authors didn't just write the words or talk theory; they *lived* them. Sure, you might find a few soundbites or steps to help you lead from within. But what you will really find is emotional resonance, space for reflection, and raw, unfiltered truth. Their stories reveal pivotal moments when their integrity was tested, authenticity reclaimed, and self-leadership became not just a choice, but the only way forward.

YOUR INVITATION TO GO WITHIN
I invite you to be an active participant in your transformation. This isn't passive reading. This is work: personal, professional, soul, spiritual, a.k.a. leadership development. Here's your assignment, should you choose to accept it:

1. **Engage Authentically:** Show up with curiosity and an open heart. These stories are meant to be felt, not just read.
2. **Exercise Your Discomfort Muscle:** Let go of the need to agree with everything. This isn't an echo chamber for what you already believe. Stretch. Reflect. Be willing to see things differently.
3. **Personalize Your Experience:** Highlight, annotate, journal, or use whatever tools help you capture what resonates. What stings. What stays.
4. **Redefine Leadership:** Explore how to bring more presence, more truth, and more alignment into the spaces where you lead and live. Ask yourself, *What does it look like to lead from within, consciously?*

This isn't a script. It's an invitation. A conversation. A co-created space for brave reflection, honest dialogue, and the big SHIFT. *Leading From Within* is your mirror, your map, and maybe even your moment of reckoning.

Think of it as your leadership Vegas—what happens here, stays here, until you are ready to share. And when you do? Do it from a place of alignment and conscious choice. Let this be your brave space. Your safe space. A sacred ecosystem for growth, awareness, acceptance, authenticity, and transformation.

The power of *Leading From Within* isn't just in these pages. It's in what you do with what meets you here.

Let's get into what it means to redefine what leadership means, for you.

PART I

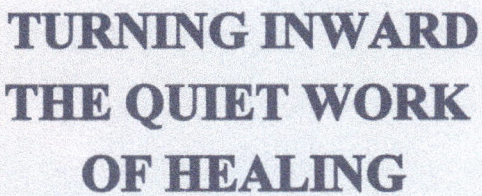

TURNING INWARD
THE QUIET WORK
OF HEALING

"You don't heal by moving on. You heal by moving in—into the pain, the lessons, the truth of who you are."

— Unknown

CHAPTER ONE

JENNIFER PIHLAJA
THE QUIET POWER OF TURNING INWARD

Iturned 50 earlier this year (2025), and I'm still celebrating! I'm halfway through a year of specific intentional moments. Because it was a milestone and celebrations are always important, and because I made it this far.

Aging is powerful. I've always admired and enjoyed spending time with older folks, not just for their stories but for their perspective. They'd seen some things. They carried a kind of steadiness I didn't yet understand, but really wanted to. Life lessons, and leadership lessons.

Leadership is forged inside. It gets confused or perceived with what people see on the outside. Leadership to me is inner work, knowing the strength and possibility of our best selves, while staying keenly aware and challenging ourselves with the work we have to keep doing on the inside to get there.

It turns out, you don't earn that steadiness by skimming the surface. You earn it by going deep; inside your body, your place, your beliefs, and your fears. Five years ago, life cracked me open. And everything that followed pulled me inward. This is the story of what I found there.

DIAGNOSIS: WHEN STRENGTH BECAME SURVIVAL
First, the cancer made me go inside.

We called it "the freckle." A small bit of cancer.

Five years ago I was diagnosed with mucosal melanoma, specifically vaginal melanoma. Mucosal melanoma is a different kind of cancer, different than cutaneous (the kind on your outside skin that they cut off).

It's less than 1% of melanomas, and found inside – your nose, mouth, eyes, your brain.

Basically cancer that forms in your innards. In this case, innard my vagina.

With this diagnosis it took a little time to determine what was happening. It was confusing, awkward, and scary. I was learning about my diagnosis from young medical folks who wouldn't look me in the eyes as they said words I had never heard before. *The Google machine* was the opposite of helpful. In one dusty, dated study, the number that stuck with me was 14%. As in, there was a 14% survival rate at five years. That number lodged itself under my ribs and refused to leave.

Quite literally, this was inside the deepest part of me. I've always known enough about my anatomy, thank you very much—my mother was a sex education teacher and we grew up in a home that used correct anatomical names for our parts and offered an array of resources on various topics, whether you really wanted and needed to know or not.

Despite knowing my parts, in the doctor drawings, I learned it's not really a straight shot up from your vagina to your cervix into your uterus. There's a meandering cranny, a fold, a little cul-de-sac at the end where your vagina meets your cervix, and the freckle was hanging out there up against the side next to my bladder. I daze-dreamed about how maybe they could just pull it out, like a specialized team could fish around with a wire and hook, or a gnarled finger, and scrape it out. It would be like something out of an 80s science fiction movie. All conversations about radiation made me think of burning lasers, and immunotherapy was incomprehensible science fiction.

Surgery was quickly scheduled. Not only to take out the freckle, but a lot of my parts, the obvious parts removed in a hysterectomy like the cervix and uterus and tubes, but even the top of my vagina, and the parts that us non-doctors might not remember from biology class like soft bands of ligaments and inguinal lymph nodes. My brilliant and kind surgeon told me not to worry; a total abdominal hysterectomy is a surgery she's done many times and she'd keep as much of my vagina "as she could." That conversation was one of the most jarring, but she shared another fun vagina fact: it's generally proportional to your height, so I had some to spare and it shouldn't be more than a bit. After decades of wishing myself smaller and feeling like I took up too much space, it was time to be grateful to be a towering woman of size.

Staples closed me up, some of those insides had been taken out, and I was reportedly on the road to recovery. It did not feel that way. It felt like it just got real, and I was really scared. I stayed in the hospital over Thanksgiving week, and I remain humbled and grateful for the folks that cared for me. The first time the nurses tried to help me get out of bed, my body was rigid, all of my muscles contracting and protective of my belly wound. I couldn't bend and didn't want to stand, and I was holding my breath and starting to panic. One of those nurse angel women held my arm and told me to breathe. "Breathe out when it feels hard, baby."

I haven't had a recurrence. This is where my inner leadership would be forged. One of my doctors told me early on that I needed to believe in being an outlier, someone for whom the known and traditional path of this disease would not apply. I've found that comforting in more ways than one. So know that I am an outlier, that I have great health care, and that I am well and without evidence of disease.

My dear friend's father, an oncology expert, told me something I carry with me. He's seen some things and has some perspective. While in the early learning days of what this all meant, he told me something very softly, as if it was very important and I needed to really, really listen. It was an observation I have come back to often over the last five years of regular scans and moments when anxiety about recurrence has consumed me. He said that there are advances in medicine and treatment and testing in this field that we couldn't have imagined 5, 10, or 20 years before, and that there would be advances in the future. We are learning more every day, he said. We can't imagine how much more we can learn about how we find and treat diseases and people.

Those terrifying 14% odds are old news. It was found early, and I'm going to continue to be fine. Those smart science people now have a blood test that I took for the first time recently, which, as I understand it, mapped the makeup of the "freckle" material and will allow recurrence to be detected early in my bloodstream. Yeah, I'm going to keep cheering and advocating for advancements in science that sounded like science fiction just a mere five years ago.

RECOVERY AND REDEFINITION: WHAT MATTERS

For many women, having children is a defining moment. The possibility and practice of being a mother and having children was what we learned from our baby dolls, as much the American girl dream as anything else. Partnered with apple pie and the Fourth of July. Expected. For me, being a mom wasn't my journey and that was determined long before the cancer or hysterectomy.

But the loss of that expectation or moment deserved holding for a while. And feeling that loss brought the want to redefine how legacy works. To be clear and reflect on what makes me a woman, regardless of what body parts, and what maternal or marital status. How being a good ancestor is rooted for me in other ways than being a mama. What impact do I want to leave behind? Recommitting to what that path looks like for me became clearer. I've got a lot of oldest daughter, big sister, compassionate friend, and fabulous favorite auntie energy, and I intend to use it for good.

The world tries to tell us a lot about what makes us women. What body parts and what maternal or marital status. Here in the middle of a revision of the same old cultural conversation about the role, value, and visibility of women who don't fit a particular definition of womanhood, I'd rather we be listening to each other, seeing our commonalities, and celebrating our differences.

I find community in raising awareness and advocacy. As my friend's dad's whisper taught me, there are advances in science we can't even imagine yet, as long as we keep investing in learning more and don't stop looking ahead. Right now, I'm fearful that we're going to stop learning and advancing. In science, and in the way we treat women with all kinds of differences.

Isolation Within Isolation: Grieving in a Global Pandemic

As I'm healing post-surgery and I begin to glimpse recovery, the world shifts again. I had been limping through the holidays, and after my recovery went through complications and upheaval, things started feeling like there was a path to the outside again. Then it was March 2020. We went inside our houses, and spent all that time inside our heads with our anxiety about the world.

I think of the pandemic as a time when I was scared to breathe, particularly in the beginning months. Scared to breathe in, and scared to breathe out. Things stopped for a while. My initial follow-up scans were delayed, first by weeks, then by months. The hospitals were full and provided essential health care only. Understood.

Predictably, the timing and my surgical recovery timeline made us exceedingly cautious about being "in the world." This let our natural homebody selves build a cocoon, with us inside, alternating between fear and horror at the events in the world, fear about my health, and projects.

In our cocoon, we had projects that helped. Connecting with family and loved ones: a project. Getting another puppy: a project. Gardening: a project. Starting Spanish lessons (for the sixth time): a project. Cleaning out the hold: a project. Puzzles (my favorite non-project projects because they always have answers, even if it takes a while to figure them all out): a project.

Figuring out what to do with this diagnosis and everything else going on in the world? Not thinking too far ahead was the project there.

You may be asking yourself, *What does it mean to clean out the hold?*

Cleaning the Hold: Space for Legacy

The hold is a room where we store stuff. My husband said it's the room on the boat where the crew stores things. We have a room in our basement that we call "the hold." It has a lot of stuff, and we did a lot of cleaning. I also had a lot to clean out of my mental hold. I had time to do some exploring and learning. Reflecting and unlearning. What did I need to clear out? What did I need to invest in? What legacy was I going to leave behind? What were the ripples?

The world went still, and I followed it inward. Cleaning out the hold became a metaphor—an invitation to sort through what I no longer needed and make room for the wisdom I hadn't yet met. The quiet wasn't empty; it was full of questions that required listening instead of fixing.

As much as I was captured, heartbroken, and angry by global and national events, riveted to the external, most of this project time was spent doing inside work. Internal, inside. Understanding, embracing, and figuring out who I was now at my core, how I could understand and use my strengths, how I showed up and held space for other people, and what I was being called to do.

The internal work was internal, but deeply inside and connected to the spiritual for me. Finding strength within involves tapping into something bigger. The connectedness of the seemingly different types of pain, and the healing that can only happen if done *both* inside and with others.

Throughout this time, I kept healing—physically, but also emotionally and spiritually. I explored the bright and the shadow sides of my strengths. I evaluated and examined my values and made some shifts. These projects were the real work, and they will continue to be lifelong work.

That inner work raised some bigger questions—the kind that don't have easy answers.

- How are our insides strong enough to take on the outside?
- What makes an individual, a team, a community resilient?
- How do we keep going, especially when everything feels uncertain??

RECLAIMING SISU: LEADING FROM THE INSIDE OUT

Part of the easy cliche of cancer journeys is that they really give you perspective about what matters, and what might not matter as much as you thought. So do global pandemics and reckonings with systemic racism, and 2020 didn't pull any punches.

For me, those pieces of life aligned in a way that connected. The deep uncertainty of those moments in my personal and our global world had connectedness. Within deep uncertainty, there's something really deep inside of us that holds us, and pushes us forward. It's in the foundational parts of our person, the parts that aren't visible or touchable, but are so very much there.

In my family's Finnish American culture, there's a concept called Sisu. Sisu doesn't have a synonym in English, but growing up it was described as "guts" or bravery, as in, "That guy, he's got guts." He seemed fearless— he's got Sisu. Stories about miners, farmers and loggers, soldiers and athletes. It was communicated as an admirable characteristic, an undefeatable strength, the ability to dig deep when you felt like you had nothing left in the tank. It also felt and sounded a lot like tough love – and I intentionally used "he" as a pronoun in the example above. There was a certain "Toughen up, remember your Sisu," often accompanied with Finnish stoicism and directness.

Sisu is something you can feel in your body, and you may struggle for the words, but you know it in your gut. Part of the updated definition I embrace for this concept is that Sisu is an action mindset, meaning it doesn't stand still; it moves and grows, and strives to make something better. Like having a growth mindset, it means we have the ability to grow and change beyond the current situation, and are not limited by what is now.

As I draw connections between my own story and others, I carry forward that Sisu means something slightly different than the definition I had for my first half of life, and it's not about the external definitions of what brave looks like. It's the internal knowing of what your own bravery feels like, and being comfortable with the uncertainty of many things. It means when I don't know the answers, can't answer the questions, and still keep moving forward with gentleness, curiosity, and in connection with others. Breathing out.

Being gentle can be the toughest thing of all in a world that rewards toughness. I prefer to see the strength and beauty in a gentler Sisu that is as strong, if not as "gutsy." It is Sisu rooted in family, community, stories, and faith that questions and wavers but keeps moving forward. It is a Sisu that shows up for other people when they need you and reminds them to breathe. It is passed to me, and I hope to leave it behind.

Redefining Sisu changed how I see myself. But it also changed how I see my role in the world. Because when inner strength takes root, it doesn't just steady you. It reshapes how you lead, how you love, and how you show up—for others, and for what comes next. It is transformational.

BECOMING THE ANCESTOR: A CALL TO LEAD DIFFERENTLY
The experiences of five years ago set me up for the second half of life in a way more attuned to my own leadership style and approach than any external motivator or example that might have been the case in the first half of life. It's not about me—it's about us.

Being a good ancestor to me means caring for and being in community with a broader community of women and all people; seeing each other, our strengths, and our stories. Those who have walked before us, and those we will never meet.

In community as an advocate, I'd like to point out that one of the reasons the survival rates were pretty dismal for cancers like my little freckle is because it has not historically been detected until advanced, and older women do not receive the same level of care. Within those statistics, like in other areas of women's health care, black and brown women have even worse odds. It's important for medical practitioners to fully see all women at all stages of our lives and our health care needs. In the future that I want for all of us, awareness leads to action on women's health care, access and treatment, and continued and expanded medical research.

I think I've been waiting a long time to grow old. To get wise and become a whisper of the crone archetype. The woman who serves as a guide. Someone who has seen some things, found a version of her own wisdom and feels worthy enough to live her life authentically. To share her story, when it's helpful, to listen to others and dare hold their hands and remind them to breathe as they grapple with their own story and circumstances.

Telling this story has two purposes. For me, to be a good ancestor and to share my story. For you to know that everything, as we think it is, can change, and it will be okay.

So yes, I went inside my body, my beliefs, my grief, and my strength. But I didn't stay there. Because real leadership doesn't end in reflection; it begins there. We do the inner work not just to survive, but to become the kind of people who lead with intention, advocate with compassion, and live in a way that shapes a legacy bigger than ourselves. I will not pass on DNA, but I hope to pass along some perspective. And if that perspective helps even one person breathe a little easier through the hard parts, then I'm exactly where I'm supposed to be and this is how I'm supposed to lead. This isn't just my story; it's ours. And we keep going, not because we know the way, but because our own version of Sisu inside us refuses to stop.

I hope we continue learning, and that the women who face a weird freckle in the future are met with even more information, and compassionate care, eyes leveled at them with assurances that they too will beat the odds.

I hope that everyone learns that they can find what they need inside of them, and that going deep will help them show up differently as humans and as leaders.

Mostly, I hope there is someone to remind you to breathe out at the hard parts, and that we're here to hold each other's hands.

We don't just lead from our strengths. We lead from our scars. And if we do it right, someone else gets to breathe a little easier.

ABOUT THE AUTHOR

JENNIFER PIHLAJA

Jennifer Pihlaja is the founder of Rowan Strategies, a coaching, facilitation, and strategic consulting practice rooted in three decades of leadership experience. She is on a mission to reshape how we approach professional development—prioritizing resilience, confidence, and sustainability for individuals and teams. Passionate about creating structure and space, Jen helps people bring their best selves and strengths to all they do.

Over the past thirty years, Jen has led with curiosity, compassion, and connection—values that have guided her through every chapter of her professional journey.

She co-founded and served as managing partner of McKenna Pihlaja, a woman-owned media firm focused on storytelling and strategic messaging. Jen also founded and directed the pilot programs for the Blue Leadership Collaborative, a paid training and professional development initiative designed to support and retain women and people of color in campaign management roles. She has held leadership roles in political organizations such as EMILY's List and the Democratic Congressional Campaign Committee (DCCC), as well as on campaigns and in government. Above all, she considers her work as a mentor and advocate among the most meaningful of her career.

Jen is a graduate of Hope College and earned an executive certificate in facilitation from Georgetown University. She is a certified Gallup Global Strengths Coach and is pursuing her ICF-PCC certification. Active in her community, she serves on multiple volunteer boards.

Jen lives in Washington, D.C. with her husband, two dogs, and an unruly row house garden, but will quickly tell you she remains a proud Midwesterner.

CHAPTER TWO

DARCI L. GRAVES
I DON'T HAVE CANCER AND MY DOG ISN'T DEAD

I don't have cancer and my dog isn't dead. That's my baseline. The refrain I repeat when life gets disrupted. When the plan changes, the bad news hits, or the universe decides to be especially unfriendly. All the things we call "the worst": a meeting that should've been an email, relentless traffic, the endless scroll of bad news. In those moments, I take a breath and remind myself: *I don't have cancer and my dog isn't dead.*

Because once, both of those things were true. And when they were, I didn't know which way was up, much less how to move through. Surviving that kind of back-to-back upheaval redefines you: your sense of self, what you can control, and what truly matters

This isn't just a story about cancer or my dog, Tessa. Not exactly. It's about how this time reshaped how I show up, navigate complexity, support others through uncertainty, and lead with intention. It's about how to keep going when everything you counted on has changed. The story starts with a dog, 16 rounds of chemo, and one unexpected comment from my niece—a simple phrase that just clicked and planted the seed for what would become a new way of moving through disruption, the art of *falling up.*

THE DISRUPTION
In August 2013, at 39, I was diagnosed with stage 2 triple-negative breast cancer. The kind that makes your doctor wince just reading the report. Three weeks later, I had a double mastectomy and reconstruction. By October, I had started six months of "we're going to kill it dead" chemotherapy. One of the drugs was nicknamed *the red devil* by the nurses, if that gives you any idea.

Then, in November, I had to say an unexpected goodbye to my soul dog of over 10 years. It was 2 a.m. She woke up disoriented, unable to walk straight. Her eyes darted back and forth. My mom and I rushed her to the emergency vet. We were told it was time. The bottom fell out.

As she lay her head in my lap one more time, I tried to stay strong so she wouldn't be scared. The last words she heard were the same ones I'd whispered to her nearly every night since the day we rescued each other:

> *I love you, Tessa.*
> *You're the best dog a girl could ever ask for.*
> *I will love you for the rest of my days.*
> *And I'll take care of you for the rest of yours.*

As I checked out—bald, weeping, and weak from chemo—the vet tech said something that still triggers me: "God doesn't give us more than we can handle." I know she meant well. But I wanted to scream. She didn't know me, nor my relationship with any God. I managed only a quiet but firm: "He is greatly overestimating me at the moment."

We went home. I cried so hard, I vomited. My body simply couldn't hold it all, not the raw grief, the fatigue, nor the rage. It came in waves that night and in the weeks to come. It was the darkest of many dark moments. But even in that darkness, I realized something had to shift. I couldn't stay in this pain forever. I didn't know how to move forward…But I knew I couldn't keep feeling like this. *That flicker, however small, was the quiet beginning of something else.*

THE START OF FALLING UP

Around the same time, my eldest niece, just shy of two, was walking with my brother near a playground. A boy fell.

> "Look at that boy. He fell down," she observed.
> "Yes, he did," my brother replied.
> "He needs to fall up," she said.

That phrase, *fall up*, clicked. It wasn't your typical refrain about bouncing back or building character. Because, *for the love of whatever you consider holy*, can we stop using "resilient" as a compliment? When I hear, "Oh my God, you're so strong, so resilient," all I hear is: "Holy crap, you've been through a lot." You know what else we call resilient? Rubber bands. They stretch when we ask, become brittle with age, then snap when overused. So why aspire to that?

We celebrate survivors, but rarely make space for the process of survival. We applaud people for making it through, but overlook the daily grief, grind, and grace it takes to keep going. Survival is the long, winding middle. It's there, where we don't need praise (or pressure) for bouncing back, but permission to just be. To process. To shift. To rebuild.

Yes, resilience is important. But it's not a trophy. In all my conversations with people navigating personal and professional trauma, I keep coming back to this quiet truth: Wouldn't we rather not have to be resilient at all?

Disruptions are inevitable. Resilience endures; falling up helps us transform. It's the decision to move through pain with purpose. It ensures stress doesn't leave us brittle or bitter. And it helps us rise, not back to who we were, but toward who we're becoming.

So, what does it mean to *fall up*? It means refusing to let hardship or upheaval define us—but also refusing to pretend it didn't change us. It's not about silver linings or "Everything happens for a reason." Some things just happen. And they suck. *Falling up* is what we do next. It's learning to move through grief without rushing to closure or bottling it up. Strength isn't stoicism. Vulnerability isn't weakness. It's having people around you who don't just say, "You are strong," but sit beside you when you don't feel strong at all.

Because here's another truth: we need to rethink how we talk about struggle and life's crappy detours. When you are down, "You're so strong" can feel like pressure. "You've got this" can feel like dismissal. And "Everything happens for a reason" can feel like betrayal. Sometimes, the kindest thing we can say is: *That is too much. You shouldn't have to go through that. You're allowed to fall apart.* We don't need more platitudes;

we need presence. We need a culture that makes space for people to fall apart, acknowledge grief, and still trust they can rise. That's what falling up is about. It's not about being a rubber band. It's about rising on your terms, in your own time. Not as the person you were before, but as someone who now knows the power of still being here.

THE ART OF FALLING UP

During my breast cancer journey, *falling up* became a practice, a series of intentions I returned to again and again – **feel, rest, plot, rise, and cheer.**

Like the stages of grief, the process of *falling up* wasn't linear. I might feel, rest, and cheer all in a single day—or in a single moment. These weren't boxes to check, but stops along the journey to becoming me again:

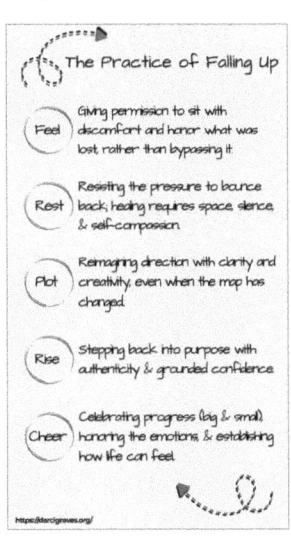

The Practice of Falling Up

Feel — Giving permission to sit with discomfort and honor what was lost rather than bypassing it

Rest — Resisting the pressure to bounce back, healing requires space, silence & self-compassion

Plot — Reimagining direction with clarity and creativity, even when the map has changed

Rise — Stepping back into purpose with authenticity & grounded confidence

Cheer — Celebrating progress (big & small) honoring the emotions & establishing how life can feel

https://darcigraves.org/

FEEL

When I found the lump in my breast, I wasn't exactly surprised. Freaked out? Absolutely. But surprised? Not really. Breast cancer doesn't just run; it gallops through my family. I always knew, intellectually, that it was possible. But there's a canyon-wide difference between knowing something in your head and feeling it in the pit of your stomach. It's like anticipating the loss of someone you love. You know it's coming. You brace. But when it happens, the ground still falls out from under you. I cried. I wallowed. I stared at the ceiling and thought, *How am I going to do this?* I knew I could. I just didn't know how.

Some days were manageable. Others weren't. Some felt fine…until they didn't. Like when I'd scream in traffic, "I have cancer and my dog just died! Get the EFF out of my way!," then think, "Maybe I'm not doing as well as I thought." Or when "Brave" by Sara Bareilles, the song that played during my biopsy (because of course it did), came on at the grocery store, and I stood frozen, hand on a cereal box, just breathing. Knowing versus experiencing are two very different things. So, I focused on what I could control: **feel, rest, plot, rise, and cheer.**

REST

Chemotherapy involves a lot of lying down, but true rest is more than naps. We've given "rest" a bad name, as if it's laziness or procrastination. But rest is progress. It's the work behind the work, the maintenance that keeps us from breaking down. We should treat rest like brushing our teeth—routine, non-negotiable, preventative. We do it not because something is wrong, but because it helps prevent something worse.

Rest is space. It's how we catch our breath, refill our cup, and steady ourselves for what's next. Sometimes, it meant protecting my energy in a system that constantly drained it—decoding medical bills that made no sense, finding new ways to sleep after surgery, or realizing that even retelling my story was its own kind of exhaustion.

No one warns you about the post-crisis crash. But it's real—and brutal. Rest was how I started to soften the landing.

PLOT

Eventually, rest turned into plotting—a strategy for how to survive and rebuild. I chose doctors who listened. I made hard but necessary financial decisions. I accepted help. I leaned on an inner circle and shared updates in ways that preserved my energy. Friends sent what we called "doses of good mojo": pears, unicorn bouquets, fuzzy blankets, and kid drawings. Their kindness didn't just comfort me—they buoyed me.

Through it all, I didn't ask myself what to do next, but rather how I wanted life to feel after. I'm a visual person and believe that words carry power. So I wrote a manifesto. My compass forward...

The manifesto became my filter. If something didn't align, I could say no. "No, thank you," and be done. That, in itself, was revolutionary to me. And I (mostly) became okay with that.

RISE

Manifesto in hand, I started to rise. Not as the person I was, but as someone who had lived through something. Survival mode is exactly that: surviving. But living again, on my terms, felt foreign and fragile. People talk about finding a "new normal," but nothing felt normal. I was in an alternate reality...living on a different timeline.

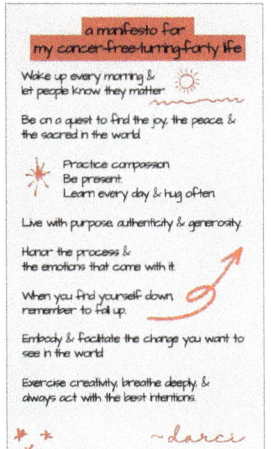

While I was still juggling doctor's appointments and figuring out who I was now, the rest of the world just… kept going. In February, I adopted a new rescue pup. I didn't feel ready; Tessa's absence was still a raw, open wound, but I realized I might never be "ready." And maybe I didn't have to be. The universe sent me Ella Jane: nine pounds to Tessa's nearly ninety, her opposite in almost every way. But she pulled me outside and out of my head. She made me laugh. She gave me joy in my everyday.

That same month, I finished treatment. The care packages stopped (as they should), but the silence left behind was louder than expected. Was I supposed to be "better" now? Normal? I had survived, yes—but I wasn't *back*. I didn't know how to explain that to people. I barely understood it myself.

Then a card arrived: "We still love you, even though you DON'T HAVE CANCER ANYMORE! Happy breast cancer awareness month, my cancer-free friend." I smiled, genuinely. My people were still there. They were just showing up in new, evolving ways.

CHEER

The last piece of *falling up* is celebrating. All. The. Things. Big or small—it does not and should not matter. After surgery, even passing gas was a win we celebrated. For some, just getting out of bed is worth cheering. When you give everything you have, you are allowed to celebrate it. Each year, I mark my *no-more-chemo-versary.* Not to relive the trauma, but to take a damn victory lap. And I don't just cheer for myself—I celebrate everyone around me. Like someone's outfit? Compliment it. Coworker crushed a project? Say it. Friend popped into your head? Send a text. Life is short. Say the good things.

AND LIFE MOVED FORWARD

That June, I turned 40 and learned I carried a BRCA mutation. Not a surprise, given my family history, but it confirmed my journey wasn't over yet. The mutation meant I was also at increased risk for ovarian cancer, the kind that rarely announces itself early. I had no interest in doing this twice. So, even though I was capital-T *tired*, in August of 2014, I chose to have preventive surgery. I knew I had done everything I could, but now I was even more exhausted.

At first, I didn't understand why I was still so drained. Chemo was over. I was back at work. But I'd drag myself home each day, exhausted. Then it hit me: in just 13 months, I had been diagnosed with cancer, undergone surgery and reconstruction, lost my soul dog, Tessa, completed 16 rounds of chemotherapy, adopted a new dog, Ella Jane, turned 40, had a second major surgery, and entered menopause. No wonder I was tired. So I gave myself grace. I made decisions through the lens of that manifesto, moved closer to friends and family, and guarded my mental health as fiercely as I had my body. I wasn't just surviving, I was living with intention. I hadn't just been resilient. I had fallen up.

FALLING UP, AGAIN

Earlier this year, I found myself repeating the refrain once again: *I don't have cancer and my dog isn't dead.* My employer announced a reduction in force. Work that gave me meaning, work that made a *difference*, gone, just like that. It wasn't cancer. But the gut punch was familiar, the same fear, a similar freefall. I thought I'd already survived. I had built a life around purpose, around service. And now, I was staring at the ceiling again, wondering how to rebuild. Again. So, I did what I had learned to do: **Feel. Rest. Plot. Rise. Cheer.** Remembering you don't need "capital T" trauma to be knocked off course. Maybe it starts with burnout. Or a breakup. Or a season of stuckness that left you questioning your next step. You just need a moment when something you counted on no longer feels safe. That's enough. That's the beginning. I turned again to the manifesto—not as a checklist, but as a lifeline. A way to find light and regain my balance…

- **Learn every day:** I set up a schedule to read, take classes, and study the things that I said I would get to "someday."
- **Be on a quest to find the joy, peace, and sacred in the world:** Art museums are my happy place, so I make a point to visit exhibits once a month. They help fill me back up.
- **Exercise creativity:** Painting, writing, crafting—something that lets me work with my hands, every week.
- **Be present:** I take breaks. I breathe. I walk. I stretch. I come home to my body.
- **Hug often:** I made a list of people I didn't want to lose touch with, and reached out.

And of course,

- **When I find myself down, I remember to fall up:** Sometimes I don't even realize I've slipped. Like slouching at your desk until your back starts to ache. Then suddenly, your body reminds you: *Hey, shoulders back. Falling up* is like that. A posture. A choice. A reminder to move with intention.

Each week, I try to live a little more of the manifesto. I'm not perfect. Some days, only Ella Jane gets me out of bed. But most days, I meet the world head-on. As I write this, I'm still falling up—still feeling, resting, plotting, rising, and cheering. But I know this much: I will fall up. Again. And I will continue to celebrate…All. The. Things.

You Don't Have to Be a Rubber Band

There is no right or wrong way to face cancer, or the loss of a soul dog, or a job, or anything else the universe might throw your way. But we do have choices in how we move forward. You don't have to bounce back. You can write a manifesto. You can choose intention over reaction. Let that be your foundation. You can define your own 5 steps or **Feel. Rest. Plot. Rise. Cheer.** alongside me. Let that be your practice. You can find your refrain—that thing you say to ground you. Let that be your reminder. I hope it isn't "I don't have cancer and my dog isn't dead." But if it is, that's okay. Being here means your story isn't over.

So, what would *falling up* look like for you…as a leader, a teammate, a friend? What would it mean to lead, not only others, but yourself, into what comes next? Find your foundation, practice, refrain, and then start falling up, with compassion and intention. It may be the most courageous thing you ever do. This is what I carry into my work, whether it's with students, colleagues, or systems trying to find their way through disruption. I don't just lead projects. I lead people through uncertainty, starting with myself.

We don't need to bounce back. We can fall up, with humor, intention, and humanity. That's the legacy I want to leave behind.

ABOUT THE
AUTHOR

DARCI
L. GRAVES

Darci L. Graves is a speaker, writer, and strategic advisor whose work sits at the intersection of leadership, equity, and storytelling. With more than two decades of experience across the federal government, healthcare, and academia, she has led high-impact initiatives in health equity, cultural competence, and organizational transformation. Known for her clarity and compassion, Darci is a trusted advisor to both senior leaders and emerging changemakers, helping individuals and institutions align their values with meaningful action.

Her philosophy, expressed in her book *The Art of Falling Up*, is rooted in both personal and professional experience. It illustrates how life's most unexpected disruptions can become defining moments of growth, clarity, and purpose. Whether navigating a diagnosis, a career shift, or a crisis of confidence, Darci believes in the power of self-awareness and intentional reflection as essential tools for leadership and reinvention.

She shares her insights through keynote speaking, consulting, and on social platforms, including on Instagram, where she can be found at @NowSpeakingDarciGraves. She holds graduate degrees in public policy, communication, and religion/sociology, and has been nationally recognized for her contributions to health equity and strategic leadership.

When she's not helping others "fall up," you can find Darci exploring art museums, photographing quirky roadside attractions, or finding unexpected life lessons in her favorite television shows.

To learn more or stay connected, visit darcigraves.org. Consider this a personal invitation to join the conversation about what it means to lead—and live—with purpose.

CHAPTER THREE

MARQUISE "BOGEY" MCCOY
FLOW OVER FORCE: LIGHTING YOUR PATH FORWARD

I used to think leading from within meant following a perfect formula for life. But that formula doesn't exist. Even as I checked the boxes: education, career, personality—I was drifting further from true success. Somewhere along the way, between the burnout, the pressure, the fear, and the facade, I realized I was following everything and everyone except myself. The higher I climbed in my career, the more scattered, numb, and disconnected I became from my larger purpose.

Not all at once. It came to me little by little, bit by bit. But in quiet, uncomfortable ways. Always when I didn't want to hear it, and the feelings always arose at inconvenient times. My spirit started whispering things to my mind that my soul already knew. Things like, "You're worth more than money—why is it the ultimate measure of success?" "If the goal is to travel the world, are we going to do it in our 70s when we're not able to move as easily?" Or my favorite repeating line, "If all it takes is money and success to be happy, then why are my bosses and the people on TV miserable?"

I believe we are all born carrying an inherent goodness. And the experiences of our life shape how we see the world, negatively or positively. Whichever way our viewpoint leans, so does our life force. Your life force is your energy. All civilizations that have existed on Earth, since the beginning of time, share this idea. Whether you call it your chi, light, spirit, or ki, it is the same force—all coming from deep within, all ancestral.

When we are born, we immediately begin taking in energy — from our parents, from our family members, and from the environments we are exposed to. We take in every little experience to every big trauma, and keep moving in our life. Depending on how volatile those experiences were, as we get older, that energy wants to come out to make room for future experiences awaiting you. Your body and brain intakes and files every interaction you have. If it's an easy experience like buying milk from 7-Eleven, it passes through without resistance. If you've experienced something heavy like child abuse, addiction, or incarceration. Those things are much harder to process quickly and you will face resistance. Resistance is nothing more than having a hard time letting go of an experience. And in the meantime, while you process your full emotions and truly move on, your body stores the experience, the feelings, and emotions related to it. We never know when these experiences will hit us, or what will trigger it, but when it happens, all else stops. You will learn that it is all in perfect timing. But in the moment, it feels like anything but that. The key is to turn inward.

When you turn inward, you will experience discomfort. It's all the obstacles you've experienced in life, built up. Sit with it. Do deep introspection on where these feelings are coming from and try to remember the first time you've experienced them, and what was going on in your life. And sit with those memories for a bit more. Offer yourself love, grace, and compassion as you come to terms with your reality. Whatever troubles your world, and whatever peace you seek, the answers can always be found within you. Try to sit with hard emotions for at least 90 seconds before thinking about anything else. Breathe continuously, and when the time expires, let it go and think about something else.

This is what it looks like to lead from within. It's not a buzzword— it's a daily choice to pause. A recognition that each day you are making choices towards your desired outcome in life. Every minute of each day is a chance to make a conscious choice to live from a place that honors your values and who you truly are – and want to be in this world.

AWAKENING OF SELF

I've heard this a thousand times: Look inside yourself. Dig deep. Meditate. Do yoga. Walk in nature. Listen to your inner voice. Yes, these practices help you get closer to life force, but there is no single answer for every person. In Spring 2024, my wellness journey ignited like a spaceship launching off of Earth on its way to Mars. I craved something different. My appetite for change was insatiable. I felt it deep within me, on a cellular level. I knew my world had to change for the better.

At the time, professionally, I faced one of the biggest transitions of my career. I had worked in-house at global technology and entertainment companies in San Francisco and Los Angeles as a corporate communications and employer branding manager, respectively. For seven years, my career skyrocketed. I was already doing well, but things really took off. I had the opportunity to work with some of the biggest names in the industry and several billionaires. I was no longer the kid in Washington, D.C., that was scared and confused when thinking about his life. I was now the man people went to for help protecting their brand, and to stand out in a noisy, competitive world. The higher I climbed, the more addicted I became to the lifestyle of fast tech money and being the man with the answers. Yet, the closer I got to higher titles and bigger teams, the more I felt myself suffocating the light within me.

What I Thought It Would Feel Like	What It Actually Felt Like
Higher titles leading to more time freedom	More time at the office and working.
More money	I bought more things to show my success. I was making more money, but I was not saving as much. The race to make more was insatiable.
Better health	The more time I spent working and vacationing, the less time I spent keeping up with my health. Doctor visits increased, along with my anxiety and bouts of depression.
Not feeling alone	No one in my family and only a couple of friends truly understood the pressure I felt inside to succeed. So I isolated myself, worked harder, ignored my health, and climbed higher.

Something shifted. My body was talking to me, but I wasn't listening. In general, I was in good health—working out every now and then, playing sports with friends once a week, and getting lots of steps in by exploring my local neighborhoods. But signs were showing up that I needed to make my life my number-one priority. I felt like I was walking around in a fog; my mental clarity wasn't where I wanted it to be. I was experiencing intense pain in my gut and a constant state of shallow breathing. It felt like I was on auto-pilot with no way to turn it off.

The key to tapping into the life-force within you is to relinquish fear—easy, right? Yes and no. It doesn't happen in big, dramatic moments but in the small choices you make every day. Each micro-decision builds into a larger one, like a snowball gathering speed. I didn't realize this at the time. When I was working in-house at global brands, I'd typically wake up in a rush. In the morning, I'd have to pack for the day ahead, my to-do list was always long, and I was ruminating between something that had already happened and something that hadn't even happened yet. Naturally, I was always feeling a lot.

One day as I was preparing to go to work for one of my busiest days, I decided to try something new, and took a moment to try meditating. One of the Employee Resource Groups (ERGs) at work had led a session on it a few weeks prior, and I wanted to try it to get ready for my big day. It didn't go as well as I hoped. I absolutely did not feel as "good" as they said I would. I felt discomfort in stillness and I judged myself for how I looked. Thousands of thoughts raced through my head a minute and every time I finally cleared my mind, a new one was in my head in 10 seconds.

All I could think about was the fight I had the night before with my partner. Tensions had risen around the lack of peace in my life. My partner was concerned about my health and mental well-being. I didn't see it as much of an issue because, in my mind, there was no stopping, just moving forward. Quitting was not an option.

I really felt like he didn't understand my point of view, especially the mental toll and tax I had to pay each day to make it through. He was concerned I was putting myself last and that I was in danger of losing myself. Deep down, I knew he was correct, but I couldn't see the light at the time.

I wrapped up my meditation after five minutes because I couldn't get my mind to stop racing. I quickly pulled myself together and headed out the door. In the midst of the chaos of my morning, I absentmindedly greeted my partner with a half-hearted "hi" and "bye." You know, the kind of exit that doesn't show them the love they deserve and that doesn't communicate "I hope you have an amazing day!" While racing to make my 9:00 a.m. presentation, I'm hastily driving and not fully present. Just as I pull into the parking garage, my phone buzzes with a text: *"Let's talk later? I didn't like the conversation we had last night, and you barely spoke to me today."*

I was faced with a pivotal choice. Would I pause and respond as my highest self, or let my emotions lead the way? I chose the latter—I reacted with everything I was carrying, like many of us do. Moments like this are defining. They're the tiny crossroads we face every day, especially when our stressors and emotions are at their peak.

Incremental progress toward your best self is always a win. And we must always remember that. What I can say is that, today, I choose my highest self eight times out of ten. For me, that's a major win! This time last year, I was at six. The year before that? Just three. You, too, can choose to make decisions from your best self's point of view, and I encourage each of us to do just that. It's what the world needs more of right now.

FEAR – Forget Everything And Run or Face Everything And Rise?

When facing fear, are you more of a *Forget Everything And Run* person, or a *Face Everything And Rise?* In the past, I would run. Today, I will face everything.

But what exactly is [1]fear? Fear is an idea that lives in our minds, reinforced by information, both true and false, that can push us forward, make us freeze, flee, or a mix of both.

If we want to overcome fear, we have to break down what we're actually afraid of. Is it fear of rejection? Fear of being alone? Fear of losing control? Maybe it's a combination, or something else entirely. Once, I had a yoga teacher break it down to me like this: "Fear is a choice. You can either choose to forget everything and run, or you can choose to face everything and rise. Only you can make the choice, but you have to

---

[1] An unpleasant emotion caused by the belief that someone or something is dangerous, likely to cause pain, or a threat.

choose a path."

We all fear something. And the more we recognize that everyone is navigating their own internal journey, the more we can show up fully and help create the kind of world we actually want to live in. Someone once told me that there are only two core emotions: fear and love. Everything else stems from those and acts as a sub-emotion.

After spending time with myself in deep contemplation, I realized that I've let fear shrink me in times I needed to be bold, make me run when I needed to be steady, and abandon ideas and dreams due to apathy and procrastination. It took me lots of painful discussions with myself and tears to come to these realities. But I also felt liberated when I made peace with my path. When we fail to recognize what's impacting us, we pass that unprocessed energy to others, often those we love the most. This in turn pushes our loved ones away, and causes us to repeat cycles of generational trauma.

There is hope. Through years of healthy therapy, hours of writing in my journal, and numerous days in deep introspection, I've learned to open up my emotions and express more. Not only to myself, but to the world. I no longer walk around with a cape of shame and a badge of embarrassment around my emotions. Now, I wear them as a marker of success. A reminder that I am human, exactly where I am supposed to be, and perfectly imperfect.

PAUSING TO HEAL

Fortunately, you can change your course. You can break generational trauma and end cycles that have repeated for centuries. Let me repeat this important message again. **You can break generational trauma and end cycles that have repeated for centuries.** It's possible! I've done it and I'm continuing to do it now. It starts with self, and with ensuring your basic needs are met: water, food, shelter, health, and mental well-being.

For many of us, this practice is difficult at first – there's just so much noise. We've been conditioned our entire lives to think, feel, and respond in certain ways. Our nervous systems are not meant to be engaged 24/7 and we are meant to have moments of pause. It's as if we're living our lives constantly being chased by a lion. I've come to realize that the constant feeling of being "on" is anxiety. Stay in it too long, and it can sink into depression. Unfortunately, I know this all too well—I spent years battling depression, even in the height of my career.

The first step toward leading from within begins by pausing. Step away from life's fast pace and sit with yourself. Go into nature if you can. Breathe and observe, and continue to do it over and over again. Notice the thoughts that surface, and how quickly they arrive, and be OK with whatever comes up. Instead of judging yourself or activating that inner critic, simply listen. Observe your thought patterns and how your emotions rise and move through you, and take mental notes. What you can do is offer yourself love, non-judgment, and kindness.

When someone first told me to try this, I looked at them like they were crazy. How could taking a moment to stop, breathe, and reflect possibly help me overcome the complex, overwhelming emotions swirling in my head and body? So I resisted. Because it didn't make sense to me, I assumed it wouldn't work.

But that's the journey of harnessing your life force. You have to sit with the chaos of your brain and acknowledge what comes up without judging yourself. In these moments of peace and quiet in nature, slowly thoughts and emotions will come to you, and all you have to do is acknowledge them and move on. It's a big shift from battling out every thought in your head and keeping score on who is winning.

It wasn't until I reached the halfway point in my yoga teacher training that I finally allowed myself to sit still and tap into this energy. The training offered me a safe space to explore my thoughts and emotions. I was given space and time to offer myself the love I knew was there, but hadn't truly felt in a long time. While sitting in various asanas and doing breathing exercises, I began to pause and ask myself, "When was the last time I felt a deep reverence for myself? Why had I lost that feeling? How can I get it back?"

The answers didn't come right away, but they did come. Through many hours of meditation and months of self-reflection, I came to understand something important: because of fear, I had trained myself to bypass my true emotions in favor of chasing joy in the moment. We must be careful not to skip over the hard stuff. When we push down difficult emotions and ignore them in favor of staying "positive," we deny ourselves the full experience of being human. Only experiencing joy is not real life for any being on Earth.

Think of yourself as a tree, and each idea you have is an acorn. As a seed, you need to give it constant attention for it to grow into a magnificent oak, rooted deeply in the Earth. Each year, it goes through seasons, and how much attention you give it determines if it survives.

Let's begin in summer, which represents the joy of your idea. In this season, it flourishes and you're excited about the potential, so naturally it grows strong. Then fall arrives, and you begin shedding your leaves. You can think of this as releasing the masks that hide your insecurities and you having to face realities of the work it will really take to reach your dreams.

When winter comes, you're fully bare and it's only you keeping your dreams alive. If winter represents those times you feel low (e.g., anxious, depressed, overwhelmed, etc.) you know how isolating it can feel. Often, when those uncomfortable emotions surface, we try to rush back to summer. And while summer is beautiful, we must also learn to appreciate our winter days just as much as our warm summer days.

Fortunately, spring always follows. And your idea made it through the winter, through your low points when you were ready to give up on your idea. You begin to see new growth and your ideas budding. Spring can symbolize the new insights and inner tools you cultivated through the winter to better support your best self. And before long, summer returns, and you and your idea are thriving once again.

EMBRACE YOUR LIGHT
I know that's easier said than done. I've had my share of battles, and

sometimes even wars, with fear. Sometimes I've won. Most times I've lost. But what I know today is this: I'm winning more days than I'm losing! When you spend enough time with yourself, you begin to understand just how complex you are. You can hold multiple feelings and ideas, sometimes conflicting, that can all be true at the same time.

Each time you sit to meditate, move your body in a way that supports your wellness, or invest in self-care, you're learning to trust yourself more deeply and the process. You're reconnecting with your intuition and keeping it aflame.

SURRENDERING TO THE PATH

Eventually, you'll reach a moment when you ask yourself, *"How do I know if this is my intuition speaking?"*

You get there by examining your "whys," and by staying true to yourself in your answers.

When you truly understand when you first realized you needed more love, or when you find grace for the people who harmed or disappointed you, you release the stuck emotions and fear that have been living in your body.

Your body opens up. Your heart and mind follow. You feel swept up by the natural flow of the universe, guiding you toward your own freedom.

You begin to sense a deep alignment—within yourself, with nature, and with those around you. Most importantly, you align with your path forward.

When you unlock the path ahead, a deep sense of relief follows. Your mind, body, and soul recognize a higher purpose, a divinity working in and through you. The things that used to weigh you down suddenly feel smaller, and actually start to propel you forward.

You start caring more about your health than about instant gratification. You realize that time with the people you love matters more than the dollars you can earn.

Your values come under a microscope, and you're left with the most important question of all: **How do you want to live your life?**

Balancing personal growth with the pursuit of a joyful, aligned life can feel complicated and overwhelming. But here's the key: remember that the valleys you walk through are just as essential as the peaks you climb.

Just like hiking, you might stumble or lose your footing along the way. And that's okay! The real victory lies in continuing forward through the valleys, toward your next peak, alongside the people you love.

And while no official system of checks and balances will confirm you're on the "right" path, take solace in this: you'll feel less anxiety and more deeply connected to your life force on your right path.

That feeling is your confirmation.

ABOUT THE AUTHOR

MARQUISE "BOGEY" MCCOY

Marquise "Bogey" McCoy (he/him) is a practitioner, healer, and lifelong student of holistic wellness. Rooted in the principles of mindfulness, equity, and ancestral healing, he is committed to cultivating peace from the inside out. Through his work, he empowers others to shine their own light by bravely sharing his own.

Bogey currently holds space for Gen Z yogis in South Central Los Angeles, where he teaches hatha vinyasa yoga, meditation, breathwork, and mindfulness. A 200-hour certified yoga instructor trained by the Tree Yoga Cooperative, he is also pursuing an additional 100-hour breathwork certification through the Holistic Breath Academy.

The name "Bogey," a childhood nickname, honors the inner child who still lives within him, and reminds others to stay connected to their own. His approach to wellness is not performative, but intentional, compassionate, and grounded in community.

Whether on the mat, in conversation, or through breath, Bogey invites people into deeper awareness, balance, and healing. His presence is soft yet powerful, welcoming yet challenging, and always rooted in love.

He currently resides in Los Angeles with his partner. You can follow his journey and offerings on Instagram: @BreatheBogeyBreathe.

Peace + love.

PART II

ALIGNMENT & PURPOSE

"Don't ask what the world needs. Ask what makes you come alive, and go do it. Because what the world needs is people who have come alive."

— *Howard Thurman*

CHAPTER FOUR

DIONNE GALLOWAY
THE BEAUTIFUL PARADOX OF PURPOSE

"The cave you fear to enter holds the treasure you seek."
— Joseph Campbell

I used to think purpose would arrive like a lightning bolt: sudden, brilliant, and undeniably clear. I imagined it would solve everything and that once I found it, things would magically fall into place: my confidence, my calling, my next steps. I'd finally feel like I was in the driver's seat of my own life, instead of lost and adrift at sea.

Unfortunately, purpose had other plans.

It didn't arrive with fanfare. Instead, it crept in quietly after what felt like too many tireless days, and a long season of buying into other people's version of fulfillment. It wasn't a single "aha" moment. It was more like learning to see in the dark. An awakening to something that had always been inside me… waiting for me to pause, stop chasing, and start listening.

What I've come to know is this: purpose exists in beautiful paradox. It is both profoundly simple and endlessly complex. It asks us to desire more while appreciating what we already have. It demands we hold hope alongside reality, embrace both the planned and the emergent, and find the delicate balance between assuredness and openness.

These aren't problems to fix. They're polarities to live. And once I stopped trying to choose between them, everything began to shift.

THE CURRENT STATE - LOST IN THE PURSUIT
We live in a world obsessed with finding purpose, but somehow, I continuously felt so immensely purposeless. Scroll through social media

and you'll see endless posts about "finding your why" and "living your best life." Bookstores devote entire sections to purpose-discovery. We've turned the search for meaning into an industry.

Yet despite all this focus—or perhaps because of it—I often felt more lost than found. Treading water with no direction or land in sight.

The modern pursuit of purpose has become entangled with achievement, productivity, and external validation. I was conditioned to believe purpose should feel like a destination instead of a journey. A noun, not a verb. I expected clarity, but purpose often reveals itself through uncertainty. I demanded simplicity when purpose lives in complexity.

I've watched brilliant, accomplished people—people like me—tear themselves apart because they couldn't name their "one true purpose." I've seen them abandon meaningful work simply because it didn't match some idealized version of what purpose "should" look like. I've experienced—and witnessed—the paralysis that comes when we treat purpose like a problem to solve, rather than a mystery to live.

I recall a time when I was my own harshest critic. When I graduated from undergrad without a clear vision for my career, I felt like a failure. After all the blood, sweat, and tears—why didn't I have it figured out?
Tensions swirled in my mind. Competing priorities consumed my thoughts. There was barely space to enjoy the success of my hard-earned degree. I felt small. I felt stuck.

It took years, and many dark moments like that, before I realized those tensions weren't personal flaws. They were polarities. And while not everything is a polarity, polarities are everywhere—pulling us in different directions.

I craved clarity in my purpose, but its truth emerged through the beautiful mess of my contradictions, shifting values, and multiple interests. I was told to dream big and reach higher, yet also to be content and grateful. Both wise, yet seemingly at odds.

Purpose demanded I cast a bold vision while staying grounded in the now. Too much hope without reality is delusion; too much reality without hope is despair.

I made plans for a purpose-driven life, only to find that purpose often arrived unannounced—through chance moments and the unexpected. I longed for certainty, yet purpose called me to stay open to new truths, unfolding experiences, and an evolving sense of self.

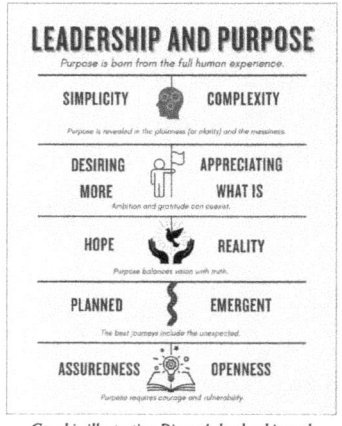

LEADERSHIP AND PURPOSE
Purpose is born from the full human experience.

SIMPLICITY	COMPLEXITY

Purpose is revealed in the plainness (or clarity) and the messiness

DESIRING MORE	APPRECIATING WHAT IS

Ambition and gratitude can coexist.

HOPE	REALITY

Purpose balances vision with truth.

PLANNED	EMERGENT

The best journeys include the unexpected.

ASSUREDNESS	OPENNESS

Purpose requires courage and vulnerability.

Graphic illustrating Dionne's leadership and purpose polarities.

These polarities aren't problems to solve but tensions to navigate. Still, no one ever taught me how to hold both without feeling like I was failing.

Of these polarities, my journey with Desiring More and Appreciating What Is, and Assuredness and Openness, proved to be the most difficult. There were times the natural tension between these poles turned destructive and threatened to break me. How could I let up or pause and appreciate what was when I was barely making ends meet and I had not secured the title I wanted? How could I be vulnerable and open when I found myself starting my career over again at 35 and I needed to prove myself? There was so much fear. Fear of being left behind, fear of failure, and fear of not being good enough. At times, it was debilitating.

This state is one of exhaustion. I was emotionally, spiritually, and physically tired of looking for my purpose. I grew weary trying to solve an unsolvable dilemma, which only added to my frustration and feelings of overwhelm and resulted in me feeling paralyzed. I was ready for a different approach—one that allowed me to navigate the beauty of these tensions and honored both my longing for direction and my need for discovery.

What Kept Me Stuck - The External Orientation

To understand why I felt so lost in my pursuit of purpose, I needed to examine what was shaping my approach to this most personal of journeys. The answer was in my external orientation—my habit of looking everywhere but within for the answers I sought.

From childhood, I was conditioned to find validation, direction, and worth through external measures. I recall grades, awards, and approval from others being real drivers of my choices because they felt so tied to my sense of identity and worth. At 13, I dropped out of the middle school basketball tryouts—something I was very excited about and had trained hard for—not because of feedback from the coach, but because an upperclassman said she didn't think I was good enough. As an adult, I contended for promotions, higher salaries, and possessions. I blindly chased things I wasn't even sure I wanted. Over the years, I became an expert at reading the room, meeting expectations, and performing—ignoring what was trying to emerge, distracted, and not honoring or revealing my authentic self. This external focus served me in many ways as I climbed, but it became a liability when I turned to the question of my true purpose.

The pursuit of purpose has been corrupted and commercialized. We look to experts, assessments, and formulas to tell us what our purpose should be instead of trusting our own authority. We compare our inner experience to others' external presentations. We try to reverse-engineer purpose from studying people we admire, forgetting that their path was uniquely theirs.

For me, this external orientation manifested in several specific ways that kept me stuck:

The Comparison Trap: I focused on others who seemed to have figured it all out, their purposes neatly packaged in inspiring updates. I forgot that I was comparing my behind-the-scenes to their highlight reel. Their clarity might have come after years of uncertainty, their confidence after countless moments of doubt.

The Perfect Picture Syndrome: I believed my purpose should look a certain way—glamorous, important, front-page worthy. I dismissed the quiet callings, the ordinary moments of meaning, the purposes that don't photograph well. I was missing the profound while in pursuit of the impressive.

The Timing Pressure: I internalized messages about when I should have my life figured out. When I was still in undergrad and searching at 24, I felt behind. At 35 when I was questioning my career direction, it seemed like I was moving in slow motion. These arbitrary timelines created anxiety that clouded my inner knowing.

The Binary Thinking: I approached purpose as if I must choose one thing, pursue one path, have one clear answer. This binary thinking ignored the reality that I am a complex being with multiple interests, values, and ways of contributing to the world.

The fear of uncertainty compounds these external pressures. We live in a culture that worships certainty and treats doubt as weakness. Yet purpose often emerges through exploration, experimentation, and the willingness to not know.

The addiction to busy-ness plays a role too. I was so caught up in doing that I rarely created space for being. Purpose emerges from stillness, reflection, and presence—luxuries that felt impossible in my overscheduled and fast-paced life. I stayed in constant motion, hoping that the right opportunity would find me, instead of creating the conditions for my inner wisdom to emerge. It wasn't until I felt the immense stillness of grief, first with the loss of my father in 2015 and then with the loss of my mother in 2021, that I really slowed down and made the space to just be.

Finding the path forward required me to learn how to hold the internal and external. It also meant learning to listen to and trust my own experience and value my own knowledge.

THE INWARD TURN - RECLAIMING MY POWER

The journey from external seeking to internal knowing began with a simple but profound shift: turning my attention inward. This wasn't about becoming self-absorbed or dismissing the wisdom of others. It was about recognizing that the most important answers could only come from within, and that I already possessed everything I needed to discover my purpose.

The inward turn required me to reclaim my own authority—to trust that I was the expert on my experience, the author of my story. This felt terrifying after spending a lifetime deferring to others' expertise, but it was also profoundly liberating.

Reconnecting with Your Inner Wisdom

I realized that my inner wisdom was always present, though it often spoke in whispers. It communicated through sensations in my body, emotional responses, energy shifts, and moments of connection or resistance. I had to slow down and pay attention to hear it though.

I'm still amazed at how loss sparked my reunion with my inner wisdom. It forced me to reopen the door, really listen to myself for the first time in a long time, and call bullshit on all the false narratives and preconceived notions I'd subscribed to.

I started noticing what energized and drained me. How I'd lose track of time when supporting instructional design. How I felt most alive when helping friends, colleagues, and eventually clients navigate challenges and uncover true transformation—a fact that had been true my entire life, even though I was just now seeing it. These revelations were all data points pointing me toward my purpose.

I also had to pay attention to my emotional reactions. How witnessing inequalities in the workplace made my blood boil. How stories of transformation and resilience moved me. How getting an executive certificate in organizational consulting from Georgetown University made me feel proud because it was aligned with something deep within me. These emotions were messengers, carrying information about what mattered to me.

Embracing the Both/And

The inward turn also requires embracing the "both/and" nature of purpose rather than the "either/or" thinking that has kept us stuck. You can be both confident in your direction and open to course corrections. You can both desire growth and appreciate where you are. You can both plan strategically and remain receptive to emergent opportunities.

This both/and thinking allowed me to hold the polarities I mentioned earlier without feeling torn apart by them. Instead of seeing these tensions as problems to solve, I began to see them as creative forces that keep my purpose dynamic and alive.

Values as My North Star

When the external loses its hold on you, your values become your true north star. Values are different from goals—they're the beliefs that motivate your behavior. They're how you want to show up in the world, not what you want to achieve.

My values include creativity, justice, family, learning, and service. Unlike my goals, which can be achieved and checked off, my values are lived daily. They provide direction without demanding a specific destination.

The beautiful thing about values is that they can be expressed in countless ways. Service can be expressed through my facilitation, coaching, and care for others. The specific vehicle matters less than my value being lived.

Creating Space for Emergence

Purpose often emerges in the spaces between—between activities, between thoughts, between exhales. Creating space for emergence means building in time for reflection, contemplation, and simply being.

This meant reclaiming my time and establishing a routine. Acts that are no easy feat and still require a lot of intention. I experimented with journaling, meditating, taking walks, and just allowing my mind to wander to find what felt right and allowed me to tap into me. It also meant saying "no" or "not now" to some people and opportunities to make space for what wanted to emerge. This proved to be extremely difficult given my desire for validation and approval, but also extremely important to furthering my journey with purpose.

Trusting the Process

The inward turn requires trusting that purpose will unfold, and that it will reveal itself through living. This trust allows you to relax into the process rather than forcing outcomes.

Trust allowed me to see that my interest in certain topics wasn't random, that my emotional reactions carry wisdom, and that my somatic responses matter. It allowed me to honor my curiosity even when I didn't know where it would lead.

When I started trusting the process, I stopped rushing toward answers and started enjoying the questions that emerged. I began to see uncertainty not as a problem but as an invitation to stay present and attentive. I realized that the journey of discovery is part of my purpose.

The inward turn is ultimately about coming home to yourself—to your own knowing, your own authority, your own unique way of being in the world. From this place, you can engage with the world from authenticity rather than performance, from contribution rather than comparison.

Practical Steps - The Way Forward

Once we turn inward and reclaim our authority, it's time to translate this inner knowing into practical action. The path forward isn't about following someone else's formula but about creating practices and approaches that honor your unique way of discovering and living your purpose.

EVALUATING VALUES AND EXPLORING INTERSECTIONS

Begin with a deep exploration of your values. Not identifying the values you "should" have but recognizing the ones that actually drive your decisions and actions.

Purpose also lives at the intersection of multiple interests, skills, and values. Instead of trying to identify one thing you're passionate about, explore the places where different aspects of yourself converge.

- **Examine Peak Experiences:** I began noticing the moments when I felt most alive, most authentic, most proud. Then I identified the values that were showing up in those moments. Looking for patterns across different experiences and life phases. I also considered times when I felt depleted, frustrated, or out of alignment and ultimately what values were being compromised. Sometimes we discover our core values more clearly by noticing when they're absent.

- **Practice Checking In:** Before making decisions, I began to ask: "How does this align with my core values?" This quick check-in can often help you gain clarity in complex situations and choose paths that energize rather than drain you.

- **Explore Possibilities:** I became fascinated with what could be possible if I combined my background in marketing and operations with my passion for learning. How might my skill with communication intersect with my desire to help people transform? Where did my creative instincts meet my analytical abilities? These intersections were where my most authentic and impactful contributions emerged.

BALANCING DESIRE AND APPRECIATION

One of the most challenging polarities in purpose work is holding both the desire for more and appreciation for what is. This isn't about choosing one over the other but about learning to dance with both impulses.

- **Recognize Gifts:** Appreciation didn't mean I needed to settle or become complacent. It meant recognizing the gifts in my current situation—the skills I'm developing, the relationships I'm building, the ways I'm already contributing. This recognition created a foundation of gratitude that made growth feel expansive rather than desperate.

- **Stay Connected:** Desire, meanwhile, wasn't about being ungrateful for what I had. It was about staying connected to my vision of what's possible, maintaining the creative tension that propels growth and change. Healthy desire emerges from love rather than lack—love for what could be rather than dissatisfaction with what is.

EXPERIMENTING AND ITERATING
Purpose emerges through engagement, not just contemplation.

- **Experiment:** I created opportunities to test my interests and hunches without making major life changes. If you're curious about teaching, offer to lead a workshop or create an online course. If you're drawn to writing, start a blog or newsletter. These experiments provide data about what energizes you and what aligns with your values.

- **Stay Open:** I approached these experiments with openness and curiosity rather than attachment to outcomes. Some resonated deeply; others provided valuable information about what didn't fit. Both results offered useful data in my ongoing discovery.

CREATING YOUR PURPOSE PRACTICE
Develop a regular practice that keeps you connected to your sense of purpose. I found it helpful to incorporate things like:

- **Morning Intentions:** Starting each day by setting an intention that connected my daily activities to my larger purpose

- **Evening Reflection:** Ending each day by considering how I expressed my values and what I learned about myself

- **Regular Check-ins:** Periodic assessments of how aligned I felt and what adjustments might serve me

- **Purpose Partners:** I fostered relationships with people who supported my authentic expression and helped me stay accountable to my values

BUILDING YOUR COMMUNITY
Purpose isn't a solo journey. Surround yourself with people who support your authentic expression and challenge you to grow. I surrounded myself with:

- **Truth-tellers:** Those who lovingly pointed out when I was not being true to myself

- **Encouragers:** Those who saw my potential and reminded me of my strengths when I forgot

- **Wise Guides:** Mentors and teachers who navigated similar questions and could offer perspective

EMBRACING THE ONGOING JOURNEY

Perhaps most importantly, remember that purpose isn't a destination but a way of traveling. It's not something you find once and then possess forever, but something you live into daily through your choices, actions, and ways of being.

My purpose will evolve as I do. What felt meaningful at 25 has transformed now that I'm in my 40s, not because I was wrong before but because I'm growing. The skills I developed, the experiences I had, and the wisdom I've gained all contribute to the ongoing emergence of my purpose.

I trust that I still have everything I need to be on this journey. My purpose isn't hiding somewhere outside of me—it's alive within me. Every moment offers an opportunity to take one more step closer to the fullest expression of who I'm meant to be at this moment.

The beautiful paradox of purpose is that in embracing the questions, we find our answers. In accepting the uncertainty, we discover our direction. In turning inward, we find our way forward. The journey itself becomes the destination, and the seeking becomes the finding.

You are already enough. Your purpose is already present. The only question is: how will you choose to express it today?

ABOUT THE AUTHOR

DIONNE GALLOWAY

Dionne Galloway is a strategist, coach, leadership development practitioner, and whiskey enthusiast with two decades of experience guiding people and organizations through meaningful growth. With a career spanning the public and private sectors, she has partnered with leaders at all levels to unlock potential, drive lasting change, and achieve individual and organizational goals.

She currently serves as Vice President of Both/And Leadership at Andiron, a leadership development consultancy dedicated to helping individuals and organizations harness the power of polarities. In this role, Dionne spearheads the evolution and delivery of Andiron's leadership and management development programs and advances Both/And as a key differentiator in the leadership space.

She is also honored to serve as the Vice President of Consumer Relations for New Dawn Distilling, a Black- and woman-owned spirits brand committed to craftsmanship and social and environmental responsibility.

Dionne's leadership is grounded in both professional rigor and lived experience. She holds an executive certificate in organizational consulting and change leadership from Georgetown University, as well as a certificate in diversity, equity, and inclusion in the workplace from the University of South Florida. A proud alumna of Howard University, she earned her Bachelor of Arts in journalism with a concentration in advertising.

Beyond her professional work, Dionne is deeply grounded by family. She lives in Maryland with her husband and two children, and believes that leadership starts at home—with curiosity, compassion, and courage.

CHAPTER FIVE

JACQUELYN BSHARAH, PH.D.
THOUGHTFUL LEADERSHIP: FROM THE ASHES TO ALIGNMENT

I stood in my bedroom, crying. It was a sunny afternoon but all I felt was darkness inside and around me. The shame. The self-judgment. The aching exhaustion of trying – and failing – to meet others' expectations. It created pain so intense my only option, I thought, was suicide. I didn't want to die. I just wanted peace from the relentless noise inside my head that told me in countless ways I wasn't enough; that I was a disappointment.

Even in that unbearable pain, my desire for life was trying to break through. It surfaced as a memory of something someone once told me, "When you have nowhere to turn, hit your knees and pray." So, I did. Not because I believed in God or thought it would work, but because the sheer depth of my pain made me willing to try anything, even if I didn't believe in it.

As I was praying – begging, really – for help, I remembered another conversation, this one with a woman two streets over who had gone through her own difficult journey. Trembling, I rose from the floor and made the short walk to her home, hoping her story might provide a path through mine. I climbed the stairs to her front porch, and knocked. No answer. I knocked again. Still nothing. Dread building, I knocked a third time. When there was still no answer, I slowly turned to leave, convinced there was no help for me after all. The defeat was so complete, even tears refused to come. Then I heard it – the soft click of a door opening. That quiet sound sparked a tiny flicker of light in me; one that, over time, has grown into a powerful life force.

A quote I came across several years ago perfectly encapsulates my journey from ashes to alignment, from barely surviving to thoughtfully leading:

> *"For every step we take toward the life we want, life*
> *takes a thousand more toward us."*

At the time, it felt less like inspiration and more like a profound truth. It also offers a powerful lens through which to understand *Thoughtful Leadership*. In just one sentence, it captures the essence of it; not in theory, but in practice. *Thoughtful Leadership* isn't rooted in bravado, control, or authority. It's about moving toward what matters most, even when the outcome is uncertain. The quote reminds us that when we take aligned, intentional steps, life meets us with multiplied possibility, support, and momentum. That's when leadership becomes more than a title; it becomes a lived expression of values in motion.

WHAT IS *THOUGHTFUL LEADERSHIP*?

Thoughtful Leadership is commonly described as a values-based approach to leadership that prioritizes self-awareness, authenticity, and aligning decisions with purpose, not just performance. It reflects the dynamic interplay between our personal values and our professional roles. It integrates identity (who we are), values (what we stand for), and impact (how we affect others). For example, a leader who values equity ensures all voices are heard before a team decision. A department head who values inclusivity may challenge a popular initiative that compromises a smaller team's effectiveness. In both cases, personal conviction informs public action. That's alignment.

But alignment doesn't happen automatically; it is cultivated through intention and action. So, how does someone begin to develop the qualities and behaviors of *Thoughtful Leadership*?

FORGED BY DESIRE

It's often thought that the first step is, or should be, a knowing one, made with clarity and confidence. I disagree. I believe ***desire*** is where *Thoughtful Leadership* begins; a wanting for something more or different than what is. Desire is an internal indicator that something inside wants to shift, evolve, or emerge.

The challenge for many of us is that we've been conditioned to distrust our desires; to see them as selfish, indulgent, unrealistic, or immature. From an early age, we're often encouraged, and even pressured, to trade what we want for what others expect. These messages come in many forms: a parent's disapproving look, a cultural script about sacrifice, an offhand comment from a teacher or boss. The wording may vary ("You can't always get what you want." "It's time to grow up and be responsible." "You should be grateful for what you have.") but the impact is the same. Over time, these refrains disconnect us from our internal compass.

My recognition of desire as an internal compass didn't come quickly or easily. I grew up in a conservative, Arabic-speaking household in West Virginia. My Lebanese father and Syrian mother wanted a daughter who was both a high achiever by American standards and a traditional woman by Middle Eastern standards. I didn't succeed at either because excelling in one left me out of place in the other, and neither made room for who I was or who I longed to become. For example, I was always drawn to befriend people who were struggling. Instead of support, I was scolded: "What's wrong with you? Why do you always bring problem-people around?" My internal drive to be helpful, to see potential in pain, was treated as a flaw.

The more I tried to be who others wanted and expected, contorting myself into expectations that never fit, the more I lost myself. That's what led to unbearable pain. What I didn't realize was that the pain wasn't because I wanted too much; it was because I had silenced the very thing guiding me toward life.

Even when desire is silenced, it doesn't disappear. It lives quietly inside of us, moving beneath the surface, always searching for a way through. That's what was happening in me when I remembered the suggestion to pray, had the memory of the neighbor's experience and knocked on the door for help. I didn't know it then, but every action I took was a manifestation of desire still alive, still working, still leading me forward.

What began as a personal reckoning became a professional calling. As I began consulting and coaching, I saw the same patterns in others. Leaders who were struggling to hear, trust, or name their desires. Different stories, same thread: longing that was buried under fear and others' expectations. What had once felt isolating revealed a gift that I didn't expect: what I thought made me different became the very thread that connected me to others.

This realization reshaped how I approached leadership development. I began to see that desire is one of the most underutilized sources of wisdom and direction in professional life. Yet, many leaders don't recognize it as such. It was not uncommon when I would ask someone I was coaching, "What do you want?" to hear, "I don't know." That uncertainty was a sign that desire had been buried or silenced for too long. To help them regain the inner compass that desire provides, I used these steps which were beneficial:

1. **Time for Reflection**
   We must set aside quiet time that is free from urgency, judgment and external noise to reconnect with ourselves. Ask yourself, "If no one else's opinion mattered, what would I want right now?" or "What would I choose if I trusted I wouldn't lose love, approval, or belonging?"

2. **Attunement to the Body**
   The body can register insight before our minds do. The mind can rationalize, resist, or deny information but the body responds honestly through energy, sensation and tension. Consider how your body responds when you think about your choices. Do you feel energized, curious, excited or bored? Our bodies can provide powerful insights into our desires.

3. **Start small**
   It is not easy to unearth something that has long been buried or ignored, so identifying small wants might be necessary, like, "I want to feel proud of what I accomplish," or, "I want space to think." Every small truth toward acknowledging what we want is a step back into alignment

It can take time to clear away the noise of old narratives to hear what's truly ours. But even the smallest spark of desire can lead to alignment.

ACTIVATED BY WILLINGNESS

Desire initiates the journey. But willingness sets it in motion.

Before I hit rock bottom, I knew I needed change but I wasn't willing. I feared what I would lose: relationships, approval, love. My desire wasn't gone; it was overpowered by fear. A mentor told me, "We don't change until the pain of staying the same becomes greater than the pain of changing." That proved true. Only when the weight of staying small became unbearable did I become ready to act.

That insight reshaped how I coach and support leaders. Willingness often has to be built because aligning actions with values can feel risky, uncomfortable and scary. Take, for example, a leader who values equity but must push back on an initiative the CEO supports. Or someone who questions a decision that appears beneficial in the short term but risks long-term harm. Willingness is what bridges the gap between what we believe and what we choose.

It often emerges quietly and subtly, making it easy to overlook at first. Yet there are recognizable signs, such as:

Asking different questions
Instead of *"What will they think?"* we begin to ask, *"What do I want?"* When I reached out to my neighbor for help, I wasn't thinking about how I might be judged. For the first time, I was more interested in how I could experience life differently. The shift in inquiry signals an inner shift in allegiance from external validation to internal alignment. I see this in leaders I coach who want to have more influence. They stop asking, "What if I ask the wrong questions or my boss gets angry?" and start asking, "How could my perspective add value to the team?"

Accepting discomfort instead of avoiding it
Discomfort shifts from something to avoid to something accepted as

a part of growth. The choice to feel instead of flee, engage instead of collapse, is a sign of willingness activated. One middle manager, for example, admitted that she didn't give consistent performance reviews because she feared saying the wrong thing. As we worked together, she gained the tools and support she needed to face her fears and recognized that the discomfort was just part of the process to become the leader she always wanted to be.

Questioning others' expectations

We start to notice the scripts we've inherited about what we should and shouldn't do, and begin questioning whether—and how—they serve us. A colleague said something that resonated strongly with me: *"I've spent my entire life trying to make myself more palatable to others."* A similar pattern showed up with one client who shared that he was tired of softening his opinions and his voice so he wouldn't be labeled "the angry black man." After a moment of introspection, he made a powerful discovery. He realized that he had taken on the expectations of others as if they were his own. As he began rewriting his narrative, he gained fuller access to his strengths, skills and lived experiences.

Willingness doesn't always arrive fully formed. Aligning actions with values can feel risky, like when challenging something that the boss supports, or pushing back on a decision that is unjust. That's why willingness often has to be nurtured.

One way to nurture willingness is to determine and focus on the "why." Why is it important to you to become a *Thoughtful Leader?* Focusing on our "why" grounds us in a purpose deeper than fear or resistance.

GROUNDED BY DECISION

Once willingness is activated, it takes a decision to ground us; to turn intention into commitment. Decision is where desire and willingness crystallize into direction. It marks the moment we stop circling the possibilities and begin to move with clarity toward what matters most. This is where change becomes visible. You start to notice shifts in how a person thinks, speaks, and responds. "I can't" becomes "I'll learn how to." "Maybe" becomes "yes." Decision is the point where desire stops living only inside and begins to shape choices, habits, and direction.

One example from my career was when I wanted to become a special assignment reporter. I didn't get selected. But instead of withdrawing, I made a decision. I studied the reporters who were chosen. I identified where I needed to grow. I practiced. Less than a year later, I was tapped for a major story, and eventually was promoted to running the division.

When we are grounded in decision, learning becomes a priority. We seek tools, frameworks, and individuals who can support the direction of our desires. The most important part of the decision isn't clarity. It's commitment. For thoughtful leaders, it's when energy is focused on movement toward the answer rather than circling the question. Said simply, it's when reflection becomes direction.

MOVED BY ACTION

Once the direction is decided, it needs movement to manifest into what is most desired. A decision alone doesn't create change. It's action that moves us forward. Action is what gives commitment its shape, form, and *results*.

We often think that we have to make sweeping or comprehensive changes, which can feel overwhelming and paralyzing. But, as the beginning quote makes clear, any step toward the life we desire is met with possibility. As a colleague of mine often says, "Small hinges swing big doors."

One of my clients, a mid-level manager in a finance institution, had a strong desire to influence strategy, but didn't think her input was valued, so she resorted to silence. After a coaching conversation, she made a decision to move toward her desire. She began having one-on-one conversations with her colleagues to assess their needs, which allowed her to be a more valuable contributor. This small action helped shift how others perceived her and, more importantly, how she saw herself. She went from quiet observer to trusted contributor, not because of a title change, but because her actions were aligned with her inner conviction.

Action can be as small as making a phone call to nurture a relationship or waking up early to engage in self-care. Action means not waiting until there is comfort or confidence. A decision for forward movement is all that is necessary. For thoughtful leaders, action is not reaction. It's not driven by urgency, ego, or the need to impress others. It's driven by purpose. Their actions are rooted in clarity; not always about what to do next, but about *why it matters*. Thoughtful leaders don't chase visibility. They build integrity. They act when it's hard, not just when it's obvious or for the sake of motion. They choose actions that align, actions that build, and actions that last. Their leadership isn't defined by how much they do. It's defined by the meaning their actions create—for themselves and for others.

HARNESSING POSSIBILITY

Referring back to the opening quote ("For every step we take toward the life we want, life takes a thousand more toward us."), it's more than inspiration. It's a valuable life lesson! It teaches that any step, big or small, when taken with thoughtfulness and intention, activates something greater. Not just in us, but around us. Consider the senior manager who, rather than staying silent to preserve comfort, chooses to voice a values-based concern in an executive meeting, altering the direction of a major decision. Or the leader who pauses a fast-moving initiative to ensure it reflects the team's shared purpose. These aren't just actions; they're signals of alignment between inner truth and outer leadership.

That's what *Thoughtful Leadership* is. It's not about already having the answers. It's about being in alignment with our values, grounded in our truth, and open to what unfolds. It begins with desire, gains traction through willingness, is grounded in our decisions, and comes alive through action. Though it may sound linear, it's not. Each part has to be revisited repeatedly.

It's not clean. And it's certainly not always comfortable. But it's real. It's human. It's brave.

Thoughtful Leadership from the inside out is about leading in a way that reflects who we are, not who we've been told to be. It's about reclaiming the quiet, persistent wisdom of our inner compass and letting it guide how we navigate the world. Because when we take even one step toward what we most desire, life moves with us. When we lead from a place that is aligned with what we value most, we don't just create impact; we create unending possibility!

ABOUT THE AUTHOR

JACQUELYN
BSHARAH, PHD

Jacquelyn Bsharah, Ph.D., is an award-winning former journalist turned organizational consultant, executive coach, and trainer. As founder of Dynamic Collaborations, she has spent more than a decade partnering with organizations to drive performance, foster engagement, and build high-impact cultures. A woman of Middle Eastern descent, Jacquelyn leads with a lens shaped by lived experience, cultural nuance, and an unwavering belief in human potential.

Her extensive experience with clients—combined with a personal journey that took her from homelessness to high achievement—inspired the creation of Learned Bravery®, a proven roadmap for cultivating the bravery necessary to achieve deeply desired but seemingly impossible goals.

Before founding her consulting practice, Jacquelyn worked as a national and international broadcast journalist for the Associated Press, where she was part of the Edward R. Murrow Award–winning team covering the 9/11 attacks. That experience sharpened her ability to ask catalytic questions, distill complex information, and operate under pressure—skills she now brings to leadership challenges across various industries.

Jacquelyn's strengths-based, research-informed approach to consulting, coaching, and training has helped leaders at all levels gain insight and move to action, especially in high-stakes, complex environments. Whether guiding executive teams or facilitating leadership development programs, she creates spaces where people take brave steps toward achieving what they most want. She helps individuals and organizations discover what they stand for, and lead from that place with clarity, conviction, and bravery.

CHAPTER SIX

MINETTA MINOR
THE GIFT OF DISRUPTION: REDIRECTION AND JOY

Another day at the office—until it wasn't.

It was my final meeting of the day disguised as a typical one-on-one meeting. I walked into the conference room to awkward silence. My manager and the human resources representative avoided eye contact, their heads down. I sat in my chair, held my breath, and anxiously waited for what was coming next.

And then the dreaded words: "Unfortunately, we called this meeting to notify you that your position is being eliminated." Wait, what?!? I had been running around all day in meetings, so how could this be happening?!

It hit me like a tsunami. The delivery was so matter-of-fact, with zero emotion.

I couldn't comprehend it; I'd shown up. I'd delivered. And still, I was expendable.

In that moment, I felt like my identity had been completely ripped to shreds.

After nearly a decade of pouring my heart and soul into a job that I loved, I was being let go.

No warning. No transition. Just a sudden, seismic shift.

I was devastated. I was confused. And more than anything, I was deeply hurt.

As I sat there, speechless (which rarely ever happens), I held the letter in both hands, wanting to scream at the top of my lungs because it just hit me. In making sure the company thrived, I forgot to invest in myself.

Not knowing what the future would hold, I did what I had learned to do in the most difficult of situations: I held my composure. I fought back my tears. I left the room. Embarrassed and humiliated, I quietly gathered my personal effects that had been thrown in a box and proceeded to be escorted out of the building while my colleagues stared on.

No farewell. No well wishes. No goodbyes.

DEPRESSION: THE QUIET UNDOING
One day I felt unstoppable, and the next, WHAM! I felt like I had been hit by a ton of bricks.

Throughout my career, I've weathered plenty of storms in the workplace. from bullying to favoritism, and fighting for fair promotions. And each trial forced me to rise, adapt, and grow stronger.

However, losing my job hit me differently; the disruption and chaos that stirred up inside was unfathomable and relentless. Negative self-talk penetrated my thoughts and slowly altered my beliefs despite me knowing deep down that what I was telling myself wasn't true.

In the days, months and years following, I have battled imposter syndrome, anxiety and fear of rejection all the while being able to land employment opportunities.

The truth is…it devastated me. My confidence was shattered. And it nearly broke me.

Maybe I was naïve, but I assumed that if I delivered outstanding numbers, kept adding value, and built high-performing teams, I was safe.

Well, you know what they say about ASSuming, right?!?

My biggest mistake? I got too comfortable. I let my guard down.

Here's what I learned: safety in corporate America doesn't exist and recognizing this truth doesn't mean abandoning ambition. It means redefining safety on your own terms by:

- Building confidence that isn't dependent on one manager's approval;
- Expanding your network so you're never fully reliant on one employer;
- Developing skills that are portable and in demand across industries; and
- Pursuing side ventures or financial independence to reduce dependency.

After a lot of prayer, therapy and self-reflection, I discovered that this quiet unraveling was actually a calling, a deep pull toward something much greater than myself. It was the same voice that would later demand that I reclaim my voice, my vision, and my purpose.

Resilience isn't avoiding disruption but adapting through it. Psychologists call this post-traumatic growth—the transformation that only happens when life shakes your foundation and demands you rebuild stronger. My disruption became the redirection that shaped my calling.

Beyond Titles And People-Pleasing

As I wrestled with the depression of job loss, I realized that my identity wasn't only tied to a title. It was also tied to pleasing others. For as long as I could remember, I was wired to serve, to help, and to overdeliver. Babysitting my siblings and neighbors' kids. Volunteering at church. Taking care of the elderly. That drive carried into adulthood, which translated into long hours, extra projects, always striving for perfection, and always saying yes.

I became the "yes girl"—the helper, the doer, the fixer. On the surface, it looked admirable. Underneath, it was exhausting. I thought leadership meant being available to everyone all the time, but true leadership isn't about self-erasure. It's about self-awareness, boundaries, and purpose.

For years I introduced myself by my position: "Hi, I'm Minetta, Senior or Managing Director at…" But when that title was stripped away, I had to ask: *Who am I without it?* That question uncovered something deeper. A role can be given and taken at any moment, but a calling? That's soul work; that's internal and divine. It's knowing your essence remains when your environment changes. It means anchoring your identity in who you are, not what you do. I finally understood that leading from within doesn't mean pleasing everyone because you never truly can. It means knowing your worth, trusting your internal compass, and choosing purpose over popularity.

This is the essence of transformational leadership—leading not through control or performance metrics, but by inspiring others to find their own worth and voice.

WATCHING MY MOTHER: THE BLUEPRINT

My mother's life is more than an example. It is the foundation of my values and the standard of how I strive to lead. As a cancer survivor and hospice nurse for 32 years, she carries herself with faith, compassion, and grace. She raised me and my siblings as a single parent, making sure that even when resources were thin, love and stability were never in short supply.

From her, I have learned resilience. Not the kind that shouts to prove its toughness, but the quiet kind that keeps showing up no matter how heavy the load. I learned integrity and how to keep your word and stand firm in your values even when no one is watching. I learned service and how to give more than you take, and how to treat people with dignity and kindness regardless of their background, title, or story.

These weren't abstract lessons. They are values I see in action every single day. I watch her serve families in their most vulnerable moments, while still managing the storms in her own life. I see her patience when others might have chosen frustration, her steadiness when others might have crumbled, and her ability to offer comfort when she is the one in need of it most.

Those lessons imprinted themselves on me. They shaped my belief that leadership is not about power, control, or the loudest voice in the room. It is about presence, compassion, and the courage to keep moving forward with grace. My mother may never have had a formal leadership title in corporate America, but she embodies the kind of leadership that leaves a lasting mark on every life it touches.

My mother's values became the blueprint for my life. As I carved my own path through careers, challenges, and leadership, I realized I wasn't just following her example, I was carrying her legacy forward. Her resilience gave me the courage to define leadership on my own terms, not by chasing validation, but by choosing impact, service, and authenticity. And with that courage, I discovered my greatest weapon: my voice. Talking was no longer just conversation; it became my superpower, the force that allowed me to inspire, challenge, and move others into action.

TALKING BECAME MY SUPERPOWER

Someone I loved told me often that I "talked too much" and should "learn to shut up." Those words cut deep and stayed with me well into adulthood. It's painful when the very people you expect to protect and nurture you are the ones who try to silence you. For years, I felt small, wondering if my words were too much, or if I was too much.

Here's what I've learned: what others criticize about you may be the very thing that makes you powerful. For me, that was my voice.

I don't fully know why he felt the need to mute me. Maybe it was about control or authority; however, whatever the reason, those words stung, and yes, they shaped me. But they did not define me. Eventually, I reclaimed my voice and even told him, "The very thing you tried to silence has now become my greatest asset."

Talking isn't noise—it's connection, curiosity, vulnerability, and courage. In leadership, it's asking the questions no one else will ask, saying what needs to be said, and speaking up even when silence feels safer. Today, my voice is my superpower.

I use it to uplift, to advocate, to coach, and to negotiate. It guides students, graduates, and professionals to recognize their worth and speak their futures into existence. I use it in boardrooms, classrooms, strategy sessions, and coaching conversations. And every time I help someone find the words they didn't think they had, I'm reminded: I no longer shrink to fit someone else's mold. I've grown into my gift.

The lesson? What people once tried to mute in you might be the very thing that makes you unstoppable. Leading from within means giving yourself permission to grow into your power even if others once tried to silence it.

Owning my voice was only the beginning. But leadership isn't forged in isolation. It's tested and refined in the spaces where others are willing to believe in you. The more I leaned into my voice, the more I saw doors open through the hands of mentors, colleagues, and leaders who were willing to take a chance on me.

THANK YOU FOR GIVING ME A CHANCE

After nearly a decade in government work with a cushy salary and pension, I took a leap into IT sales, an industry I knew nothing about. A mentor, divinely placed in my life, opened my eyes to new possibilities. After prayer and many coaching sessions, I landed a position at one of the top software companies in the world. Within two years, I was promoted into leadership and went on to lead a successful team, but leadership demands risk-taking. I later declined a six-figure salary to launch my own business because I knew my assignment was bigger than comfort.

When fear knocks, faith answers. Every time I've chosen courage over comfort, God has swung open doors I didn't even know existed.

Leadership is not a solo journey. It is a shared one. Every opportunity I have been given was because someone somewhere believed in me enough to extend a hand, open a door, or simply say, "I trust you." To those who gave me a chance, thank you from the bottom of my heart.

You gave me space to grow even when I didn't yet see my own potential.

You allowed me to lead even when my voice was still finding its strength. You entrusted me with your confidence, your vulnerabilities, and your life goals and that has been the greatest gift of my journey.

I know now that leadership is not measured by titles or accolades but by the chances we give one another. Each chance I was given became not just a responsibility, but an invitation to rise. And every chance I've had to lead has only deepened my commitment to give that same gift to others.

So to everyone who gave me a chance, you are part of this story. You are part of my legacy. And it is because of you that I lead from within.

FOUNDING MY COMPANY: THE DIVINE ASSIGNMENT

People often ask how Guiding Future Success, LLC was born. The short version? I lost my job.

At first, I questioned whether I could step into this divine assignment. One born out of loss, uncertainty, and reinvention. Building a business is not for the faint of heart. It can be isolating, unpredictable, and overwhelming. But I refuse to give up because I know this is my life's purpose. Leadership, I've learned, is about listening, keeping faith, and moving forward even when fear tries to hold you back.

Looking back, I see how every door opened and closed, every challenge endured, and every voice that tried to quiet me was actually preparation for this moment, for who I am today, and for those I've been called to serve. What once felt like rejection was, in truth, redirection.

And the part that brings me the most joy is knowing that this new assignment was God's way of redirecting my path and purpose. It grew out of the privilege of leading and learning alongside an amazing and unforgettable team. People who trusted and still believe in me to coach and guide them through pivotal life and career moments for over a decade now. Their belief in me, combined with the unwavering encouragement of my son and the perspective I've gained as a business owner, has shaped this next chapter of my journey.

Guiding Future Success is more than a firm; it's a movement. It's God's vision for it to become a launchpad for every person who's felt overlooked, underprepared, or underestimated. We don't just help people land jobs. We help them find themselves and navigate their life's journey.

And every time an employee says, "Thank you for taking a chance on me," and, "You believed in me before I did"...I know exactly where I'm supposed to be.

Legacy: The Leader I Hope To Be Remembered As
These days, I often think about legacy. Am I building something that will outlast me? What seeds am I planting for the next generation to harvest?

Not all leaders are created equal. Along my journey, some managers inspired me while others belittled me. Some saw my potential while others saw me as a threat. Each interaction good and bad shaped my vision of the leader I choose to become, and the leader I hope to be remembered as.

For me, legacy isn't about titles, accolades, or even the roles I've held. It's about impact. Did I leave people better than I found them? Did I model grace under pressure, courage in uncertainty, and integrity when it mattered most?

That's what conscious leadership is: leading with awareness, presence, and purpose. Conscious leadership requires us to lead from awareness, not autopilot—from presence, not performance. My Leadership Legacy Letter is my offering to those who will rise after me. A reminder that the truest measure of leadership is not power, but the lives you empower.

Dear Future Leader,

You don't have to have all the answers to lead just a willing heart and the courage to show up.

Lead with integrity, not ego. With love, not fear. Let your boundaries be clear and your compassion fierce.

Speak your truth, even if your voice trembles. Listen with empathy, not just for the words, but for the silences in between.

Choose purpose over performance. Service over spotlight. And when in doubt, return to your why, because it will guide you when the world gets loud. You were never meant to lead like anyone else. You are here to lead like you. From within.

And never, ever dim your voice. Because someone is waiting to be seen, heard, and inspired by the very story you once thought was too much to tell.

Keep going. Keep rising. And when you feel tired, remember: this isn't just about where you're going. It's about who's coming behind you.

IN LOVE, COURAGE & FILLED WITH LEGACY,

Minetta Minor

HERE'S TO: "NEW VISION. NEW MISSION. NEW ASSIGNMENT."

ABOUT THE AUTHOR

MINETTA
MINOR

Minetta Minor is the founder and CEO of Guiding Future Success, LLC, a coaching and consulting firm dedicated to empowering students, recent graduates, and young professionals. She helps clients navigate the ever-evolving job market with clarity and confidence. Through personalized coaching, strategic guidance, and an unwavering belief in each client's potential, she transforms career confusion into empowered action.

With over thirty years in corporate recruiting, global sales, and executive leadership across both public and private sectors, Minetta offers a dynamic blend of business acumen, strategic vision, and people-first leadership. Her career spans roles as Corporate Recruiter, Managing Director, and Senior Director of Global Sales Development, where she built high-performing teams, elevated emerging talent, and advanced inclusive workplaces in industries ranging from technology to staffing.

She is an Associate Certified Coach (ACC) through the International Coaching Federation (ICF) and holds an associate degree in business administration from Northern Virginia Community College. She is also a licensed Realtor® in Maryland and Virginia, helping clients find their next home, as well as their next professional step.

Minetta has guided countless graduates into competitive internships and full-time roles. Known for pairing strategy with empathy, she equips her clients with the confidence and tools to pursue their goals with clarity and intention. She volunteers with her church, the Fairfax County Juvenile Justice System, and other organizations offering thoughtful support and compassionate leadership. Outside of work, Minetta enjoys travel, movies, and spending time with her family, especially her son, Isaiah.

To learn more, visit www.guidingfuturesuccess.com.

PART III

AUTHENTIC LEADERSHIP IN ACTION

"Authenticity is the daily practice of letting go of who we think we're supposed to be and embracing who we are."

- Brené Brown

CHAPTER SEVEN

CARL MOSBY III
THERE'S A RHYTHM, MEASURED POWER

"I've never felt more disrespected in my life, bro. There's no way
I can let this slide." — Close College Friend

The music was so loud you could feel it, and the positive energy of the crowd that night pulsed, but hearing the pain in my friend's voice as he spoke was all I needed to act. Eighteen years of learning what being a loyal friend meant and, to me, a leader, led me to rally my crew and confront the people who wronged him.

Days earlier, they broke into his dorm room and stole his things. And now, bold as ever, they had the nerve to show up to a college party wearing his clothes. It wasn't just disrespect; that was a direct challenge. To me, that could not go unanswered. This could, in fact, not slide.

Fueled by emotion and a warped sense of justice, I led the group into a confrontation that escalated until a gun was pulled. The moment that weapon came out, the group scattered in every direction. I looked left, right, and behind me, and there was only one friend (not the one whose clothes had been stolen) standing there with me as we stared down the barrel of a gun. Cooler heads eventually prevailed, no one got hurt, and we went our separate ways. In that moment, I felt abandoned; betrayed, even. I couldn't believe my closest friends wouldn't stand with me. I questioned their loyalty.

I still revisit that moment. It is one of the clearest leadership lessons of my life. I now see how I failed, not because they didn't follow me—because I never should have led them into that situation in the first place. I let my emotions decide. I created false expectations about what loyalty looked like. Most of all, I didn't protect the people I claimed to care about. That was not leadership. That was ego.

Real leadership is not charging into danger to prove a point. It's keeping people safe. It's knowing when to act and when to de-escalate. That night, I was not ready to lead.

There are endless images, movies, and stories that paint strong leadership as loud, physical, and commanding. It's rarely celebrated when it shows up as calm, stillness, or service. Over time, I've learned that some of my strongest moments as a leader have come not when I was the loudest in the room, but when I slowed down, listened, and truly showed up for the people I was responsible for.

I thought power came from intensity. That belief nearly got my friends hurt. I led them into danger. I recklessly thought leadership meant action. That moment became a turning point. Real strength would have been slowing down, protecting my people from harm, not walking them toward it.

I've come to understand that leadership rooted in service is far more powerful. Vulnerability, patience, and the willingness to listen create space for real connection. That's the kind of leadership people trust. There's peace that comes with that kind of leadership. It's not performative. You don't have to posture or shout. You show up consistently, with humility, empathy, and clarity about your purpose.

Like Jay-Z said, "No one will fall because everyone will be each other's crutches." True synergy doesn't come from authority or bravado. It starts with trust. And trust starts with how you show up as a leader: calm, consistent, and in service of the people around you. Leadership, at its best, isn't about being the star of the show; it's about setting the tone, holding the standard, and clearing the path for others. It's about knowing when to speak, when to listen, when to push and when to pause. And most of all, it's about creating space for others to shine.

Leadership, like music, has a beat. Over the years I've learned to hear it not just for myself but for the people who have trusted me to keep it. This reflects that rhythm.

THE STRENGTH OF VULNERABILITY

Some of the strongest bonds I've built have come from moments where I allowed myself to lead from a softer place. Not as in passive or lacking direction. I'm talking about vulnerability. Making space to genuinely connect with people, not just managing them.

The more comfortable I've become with the full range of who I am, the better I've been able to lead. When I stop trying to be impenetrable and instead focus on listening, learning, and understanding what drives the people around me, everything changes. I'm able to move past surface-level leadership and into something more honest. More human.

As I've stepped into bigger roles throughout my career, I've had to confront the reality that imposter syndrome doesn't vanish with new titles. No matter how much confidence I have, or how often I've been affirmed by family, friends, mentors, colleagues, or even by the results that got me to where I am, there is still a voice that sometimes whispers, *YOU haven't earned this yet.*

There is duality there. On the healthy side, it's humility—the sense that leadership is a responsibility, not a reward. That keeps me grounded, never too comfortable or entitled. But there's also doubt. Left unchecked, it can turn into a problem not just for me, but for those I'm called to lead.

Unchecked self-doubt narrows your vision. It turns your focus inward when it should be directed outward. You start scanning your flaws instead of scanning what your team needs. You spend time overthinking instead of guiding, encouraging, or advocating. There is a difference between reflection and rumination.

What I remind myself of, especially on those days when I feel the weight of leadership: I've been elevated. I've been chosen to lead. Whether by decision, circumstance, or merit, I've been placed in a position where others are looking to me for direction, clearness, support, and belief. So,

I try my best to meet that responsibility with resolve.

Even when I doubt myself, I lead—not by ignoring fear but moving through it. I've learned that helping someone push through their limits quiets my own inner critic. And those same people end up helping me, not through affirmation, but through shared progress and small wins we build together.

I belong here not because I'm perfect—because I care. I'm committed to the work. Leadership isn't being the most confident person in the room; it's showing up when it matters most. People rise when they feel seen. When they know you're not just giving orders, but in it with them, aware of their strengths, values, and motivations. That takes effort. It takes listening. It takes self-awareness to quiet your ego and humility to understand what moves others.

I've seen what happens when leaders confuse fear with respect. They refuse to admit mistakes or mistake control for influence. That kind of leadership disengages people. It minimizes their potential. True leadership reflects humanity, not hierarchy. Titles grant access, not trust. When people feel understood, they commit. When you invest time in knowing their story, alignment happens naturally.

Leading with empathy doesn't only build better teams. It builds real relationships. When people feel respected, they expect more of themselves and others.

"Lead by example" sounds cliché. But when the example includes vulnerability, accountability, active listening, heart-led decision-making, that behavior cascades. Not because it was mandated—because it was modeled.

Measured Power

My understanding of power has evolved with time, with experience, and with the lessons that can only be learned the hard way. Early on, my view of power was shaped by movies that celebrate dominance, the environments I grew up in, and expectations placed on young boys to lead with force. Power, in that context, was all tempo—no tone. Loud, fast, aggressive. If you weren't setting the pace, you were left behind. Back then, I thought power looked like what I tried to wield that night at the party. My friend had been disrespected, and I was convinced the only appropriate response was confrontation. No pause. No dialogue (maybe angry dialogue). Just action. I walked in with clenched fists, thinking that was leadership. What I know now is that I wasn't setting the rhythm. I was off beat, out of sync, playing noise instead of music.

That wasn't power. It was ego, drowning out my judgment. That was pride, cranked up, with no regard for harmony.

True power, I've learned, is balance. It's timing. It's knowing when to lead and when to listen, when to hold the note and when to let the band shine.

Power is multiplicity—the ability to gather distinct voices, divergent goals, and shape them into shared purpose. It's creating harmony from complexity.

Harmony doesn't happen by accident. It feels good. It requires a leader who understands the rhythm of the room and who's willing to adjust on the fly. You don't keep playing louder when things go off track; you tune your instrument, you shift tempos, you lock in. That's leadership.

In my career, I've found the deepest sense of purpose not in having authority, but in using my influence to advocate. That's when I feel most powerful. Not when I'm in front, but when I'm helping someone else find their voice. When I'm listening carefully enough to know what they need and respond with intentionality. Creating opportunities builds trust. And when people feel trusted, they play in sync. They lean in. That's how community is built.

Power isn't your solo. It's helping the full composition rise—your team, their families, future collaborators, and the culture you shape. The song emanates further than the stage it starts on.

But every good piece of music has tension. Being a servant leader doesn't mean fading into the background. Sometimes, leadership requires you to change keys. To cut through the noise with clarity. Sometimes, you must bring the hammer. Not to dominate—to signal the downbeat. To protect, to course-correct, to make space for others to come in on the right note.

I'll share an example. I was hiring for a role on my team and identified the perfect internal candidate. He had been with the company for years and had been overlooked more than once. He was smart, capable, and deserved an opportunity to prove it. I saw him. I knew what he could bring. And I made him a compelling offer to join my team. He accepted. And almost immediately after, I received a message from his current manager. They were disappointed that I hadn't given them a heads-up before making the offer. Which, on some level, was fair. However, if you're truly invested in someone's growth, you don't get caught off guard when an opportunity finds them. You help create those opportunities for them. That manager didn't advocate for him the way he deserved.

So, I responded. I let them know I understood their frustration, but I had no regrets. I was doing what they should have done. I felt proud to be doing so. And that hire? One of the best I've made. Not just because of the impact he had—because of what it symbolized: the choice to let the right voice be heard. That's what leadership is. That's what power is.

Sometimes leadership means going off script—knowing when silence speaks louder, or when to come in with the crescendo that wakes the room.

Measured power isn't about playing every instrument. It's about reading the arrangement. Leading from the podium when needed and stepping back to let others take the solo. The most unforgettable moments aren't solo acts—they're when the whole band locks in, playing something bigger than themselves. Wielding influence solely for personal gain distorts leadership like Dorian Gray's hidden portrait—polished on the surface, decaying underneath. Leadership becomes legacy only when it's shared.

That's the power I believe in now.

THE PRINCIPLE OF ACTIVATING OTHERS

I've worked with a lot of leaders—different styles, different personalities—and the best shared one key trait. They could identify potential in others and felt a deep responsibility to activate it. Sometimes activation happens through big, visible actions like mentorships, promotions, high-stakes decisions. Often, it shows up in quieter ways. One-on-one conversations, simple questions, a moment of attention when they see you as more than the role you're in.

I've had those moments. Conversations with skip-level leaders who, whether they knew it or not, flipped a switch in my mind. They made me believe that not only could I achieve the career goals I had, but that I *should*. That I was already capable and needed to start acting like it.

Every milestone I reach opens a door for someone else. That's multiplicity. Leadership should move through you, not stop with you.

One of the most pivotal moments in my career came when I received an external job offer for a leadership role. I wasn't in leadership at the time. I was an individual contributor who hit a ceiling I didn't know how to break through. I wanted to lead, and I was ready, but I couldn't see a realistic path within my current company. Out of transparency and respect, I let my leadership team know about the external offer. In response, I had to meet with one of the senior leaders at the company.

I walked into that meeting thinking it would be routine. It wasn't.

He asked me a simple yet pointed question: "Why haven't you told anyone you want to move into management?"

I didn't have a good answer. I had been waiting for the opportunity to find me instead of advocating for it. He told me something I've never forgotten, and it completely changed how I approach career decisions for myself and others. He said:

"By not asking the question, you've robbed yourself of the chance to get the feedback you deserve. When you ask, one of three things will happen:

- You'll get the job you asked for.
- You'll get real feedback about what you need to do to earn it.
- You'll get no feedback at all, which tells you it's time to leave."

That hit me hard. It was exactly what I needed to hear. He wasn't trying to sell me on staying. He was pushing me to advocate for myself. He activated me with truth and clarity. And in the same meeting, he offered me a leadership role. That offer changed the trajectory of my entire career. It put me on a new path, one I continue walking to this day. More than the job itself, what stuck with me was how he led at that moment. He saw something in me and made the choice to pull it forward. He could have let me walk away. Instead, he helped me walk forward. That is what activation looks like. From that day on, I made it a personal mission to activate others every chance I got.

Sometimes that means standing firm, even when it's uncomfortable. I remember hiring for a role where I had no doubt who the right candidate was. They had the talent, drive, and character to make a real impact. When I brought it up to my manager, I was met with biased and disappointing feedback. The candidate wasn't what he had in mind for the role for reasons that had nothing to do with performance or potential. It would've been easier to fall in line. To keep the peace. But leadership isn't about avoiding tension. It's about doing the right thing, especially when it's uncomfortable.

So, I trusted my gut. I made the hire and stood by it. That decision created an opportunity for someone who genuinely deserved it, and it turned out to be one of the best hires I've ever made. In fact, in both cases, I wasn't just rewarded with strong additions to the teams I was leading—I was rewarded with the privilege of watching two people grow into their full potential.

To play a part in someone's transformation is one of the most meaningful outcomes of leadership. It reminds me that good hiring isn't about filling a role. It's about recognizing talent, creating space, and doing your part to help someone step into what's next.

A true leader chooses conviction over comfort. You don't lead by keeping people at ease—you lead by doing what's right and creating a culture of growth. Leadership is a daily decision to activate those around you. Not to look good, but because the work is bigger than you. The mission is bigger than any title.

The impact you make on careers, on people, on lives will always be what lasts.

FINAL REFLECTION: THE COMPOSITION OF LEADERSHIP
Leadership and music are a natural connection. Not music that invades your ears—the kind you can't help but feel. It's the rhythm that holds everything together, even when the notes change.

That's how I try to lead.

Riding the rhythm of leadership requires reading the room with emotional intelligence. It's how we show up, make decisions, and link with people. Picking up on the tempo of what's happening, what's being said, what's being felt, what's being avoided, and adjusting in real time to stay in sync.

I don't believe in rigid playbooks or pretend every situation can be solved the same way. Teams are made of people, not machines. They change. They evolve. And so should the way you lead them.

One thing never changes: the expectation is always excellence. That's the baseline (bassline). The standard. It's the drumbeat beneath every conversation, project, setback, and win. I won't compromise on that. But how do we get there? That's where rhythm matters.

Album of lyrics from "Follow The Leader" by Eric B. and Rakim

Sometimes, things fall out of sync. A miscommunication, a missed goal, a breakdown in trust. When there's a shared commitment to doing the right thing and communicating with clarity and honesty, it's never too difficult to get things back on beat. Leadership is not perfection. It's knowing how to recalibrate, redirect, and re-center the team when needed.

In those moments, the tone I set matters. If I panic, they will too. If I bring grounded focus, they will follow it. I do my best to bring humility, consistency, and courage into the room. That combination gives me staying power.

Not every decision I make will be popular. Not every direction will be easy to understand. When I lead with principle and stay aligned with our team's values, the results speak for themselves.

The best leadership doesn't shout or perform. It sets a tone others trust, and carry. It moves like music. It flows with purpose. When it's done right, it doesn't just lead, it lifts.

I still think about that night at the college party. I've dreamed it, relived it in flashbacks and goosebump moments—wondering how one decision, one word, one misstep without grace or restraint could've changed everything. For my friends. For all of us. That truth stays with me: *everything can change with one decision.*

That's why I carry the weight of leadership the way I do. That's why I take so seriously the responsibility not just to make good decisions, but to make *right* ones with clarity, empathy, and a forward-thinking view of how those decisions ripple beyond me.

It's never just about *me*. It's not even just about my team. It's about the people they go home to. The people who count on them. The future opportunities that open or close based on how we lead in the present. Leadership is not a self-contained act. It radiates. It spreads. It echoes.

So I move with intention—not just to lead, but to protect. Not just to drive outcomes, but to center people in them. I aim for the right chord, balancing executive expectations without dimming my team's light. The business gets what it needs, but in a way that elevates those doing the work. The ones who deserve to be seen, heard, and recognized.

It's like conducting a chorus. It's layered. It's timing. Harmony. Presence. Precision. It's knowing when to come in strong and when to let others take the lead. It's giving space for the soloist and strength to the section. And above all, it's about moving people emotionally, spiritually, and collectively toward something bigger than themselves.

So the real question every leader must ask is: Can you lead your chorus to a fever pitch—one that moves people to their feet, raises goosebumps, brings tears not from sorrow, but from the awe of witnessing something true? Can you bring your team to that moment?

If you can—if what you've built is so aligned, so alive, so electric that people can't help but respond. Then you're not just leading.

You're igniting something. You're shifting the room. You're leading with power.

ABOUT THE AUTHOR

CARL
MOSBY III

Carl Thomas Mosby III is a solutions engineering leader, trusted advisor, and lifelong student of technology, people, and growth. He has built a career helping teams make better technical decisions while building stronger relationships—creating consistent partnerships between vendors and customers.

Carl has led high-performing teams across North and Latin America, advised Fortune 500 clients on cloud security and fraud prevention, and helped shape go-to-market strategies for some of the most impactful technologies in the AI and cybersecurity space. Whether building scalable engagement plans, mentoring future talent, or navigating complex enterprise accounts, he brings a sharp focus to listening, learning, and delivering value.

Before joining F5, Carl held impactful roles at Shape Security, Akamai, Verisign, and Texas Instruments, gaining hands-on experience with everything from Windows server architecture to bot defense. His leadership is informed by a commitment to equity in tech; as the global chair of F5's Black employee resource group, he has worked to ensure more voices are heard and valued at the table.

When he's not solving big challenges or mentoring future leaders, you'll likely find Carl spending time with his wife, daughter, and husky—cooking in the kitchen (occasionally with his mom), grilling outside with his Keveri, or fine-tuning his vinyl record system—because sound matters. His audiophile passion is one passed down from his dad, and it's something they continue to share today.

CHAPTER EIGHT

ASHLEY B. STEWART
FROM PERFORMANCE TO PRESENCE

Opening Prayer: Lusby, Maryland

I grew up in Lusby, Maryland, a small rural town nestled between the Patuxent River and the Chesapeake Bay. A place where people called each other "cousin" whether they were blood or not, where history lingered thick in the air like humidity, and the land itself carried memory. Lusby wasn't on the way to anywhere else. It was a shoreline world with deep roots, with churches tucked off dirt roads, and unspoken codes about who belonged where and when.

As a small child I knew hunger, not metaphorically, but physically. Sugar water filled chipped cups, and ketchup sandwiches were folded by hands that had known too much work. I remember second grade, sitting in class with my stomach growling so loudly I was sure the other students could hear it. I learned early how to suppress appetite, how to distract myself from the ache with achievement. If I could be smart enough, helpful enough to the teacher, more responsible than my classmates, maybe I would become someone who didn't feel the void.

But even in a place defined by poverty limits and racial divides, the women in my family managed to stitch miracles into the seams. My grandmother scraped together money to send me to youth leadership conferences across the state and one time as far as Arizona. My mother stood tall in her pride every day at a job that drained her spirit but could never diminish her faith. Their sacrifices wrapped around me like a second skin, shaping the edges of my imagination before I had language for ambition.

I had asked for a CD player for my birthday, an honest request for something I longed for but knew was out of my mother's reach. The morning of my

10th birthday, in late spring's humid embrace, my mother's boyfriend woke me before dawn, an unusual occurrence, because I was a pretty self-sufficient child. With an extension cord, he whipped me again and again, cursing and yelling not to "get too big for my britches." The welts rose like winding creeks on my ashy Black legs. I hid them beneath jeans that day at school as the June heat soared, making recess very uncomfortable. That brutal punishment taught me silence and shame, to hide desire and to disappear when spoken truth threatened pain. I vowed then to escape this town, that house, the weight of unfulfilled longing.

CALL TO WORSHIP: A PREACHER IN THE MAKING

I was supposed to be a preacher. That's what my mother declared over me hours after she gave birth to me. And many people in the community grew to agree with this prophecy. With strong skills in oration and public speaking, I spoke all over the country as a young person, reciting scriptures in churches and delivering speeches for school programs. In my pre-teen years, the head usher invited me to recite Dr. Martin Luther King Jr.'s final speech for Usher's Day at Eastern United Methodist Church. I stood in that sanctuary, surrounded by elders dressed in white gloves and pressed suits, and I gave them everything I had. When I reached the line, "I've been to the mountaintop," I hurled my body to the floor, mimicking Dr. King's assassination, but something unexpected happened. As the church erupted in applause I began to weep. I wasn't acting anymore. In that moment, I understood something I couldn't yet name: *Black men who speak the truth die.* I knew then that leadership could cost you your life. I didn't have the words for it yet, but I felt it in my bones.

CONFESSION: I KNEW I DIDN'T FIT THE FRAME

I would carry that knowing into every room I entered from then on. Not just the memory of that Sunday, but the visceral reality of how power, visibility, and Blackness live inside my body. I knew by middle school that I didn't quite fit the frame. I moved differently. Spoke with a softer voice and kind presence that made elders nod with approval and other little boys watch me from a distance with side eyes. No one told me to leave, but everyone seemed to know I would. I think my mother knew it too, though she held on to hope. She wanted me to attend college in Baltimore City, just a two-hour drive north. She wanted me nearby, somewhere she could reach me. By the time I was a teenager, I had already begun to outgrow the possibilities around me. I had learned that excellence was the price of safety, so I learned to perform. I learned to make myself smaller and more impressive at the same time. I became fluent in what the world rewarded.

DEVOTION: THE MASK FULLY ACTIVATED

That fluency took me far, first to Morehouse, where I was surrounded by the legacy of Black male excellence, then on to the Harvard Kennedy School and then to Georgetown, where my presence was both a signal and a strategy. I knew how to code-switch before I had language for it. I knew how to posture before I understood what embodiment meant. The mask looked like ambition, but it was really protection. It wore a well-cut suit. It gave keynote addresses. It sat on panels and answered questions with poise. People called me polished. Exceptional. Articulate ("You speak so well."). They meant it as praise. What they didn't know was that the polish came from pressure. The articulation was grief in disguise.

During my first year at Harvard, I was one of only three Master in Public Policy students admitted without prior work experience, and one of a handful of Black students in a class of more than 270. The stakes felt enormous. The university hosted a large clambake to celebrate the school's anniversary. I had never been to a clambake before, let alone met anyone from the Kennedy family, whose portraits hung in my grandmother's house beside images of Dr. King. By sheer luck, I won a student raffle to attend the event.

I showed up as I was, in my best, still with holes in the seat of my pants and worn soles on my shoes. I was painfully aware of how I looked and felt out of place, but I was not going to pass up this opportunity for a free meal and the opportunity to get up close to "political royalty." As I found my seat at the table in the middle of the tent with sight lines to every living Kennedy, a second-year student looked at me and said, "Oh, you must be Ashley. Here's your name tent. Welcome to the table. Your mother must be so proud of you."

I blinked and then froze with my mouth wide open.

That comment landed hard, a mix of surprise, shame, and disbelief. What did she just say to me at this table full of strangers? I didn't know this White woman, and she didn't know me. However, after her "welcome," my trauma response kicked in immediately. Instead of pushing back or expressing how those words felt like a microaggression, I found myself agreeing, nodding, and fawning. All evening between the buttery cobs of corn and never-ending lobster rolls, I genuflected to her and the other people at the table instead of holding my ground.

At that moment, my mask was fully activated. The little boy from Lusby who was told "you ain't shit" whispered loudly inside me. I became small, compliant, and invisible all over again, a survival tactic I had honed since childhood.

That evening was a turning point. It revealed how deeply my need to perform excellence, and not speak my truth, was entangled with fear, shame, and the unspoken rules I learned growing up. It wasn't that I didn't belong. I had learned to survive by believing I didn't.

Sanctuary of the Body

My survival strategy became precise. I crafted a version of myself that was acceptable, accomplished, and impressive. I got good at being what people needed me to be. I studied the codes. I mastered the script. I became the leader who could move between boardrooms, classrooms, and pulpits with ease.

But beneath the polish, there was pain.

Performance as a strategy to avoid my pain took its toll on my body and soul. Twice, I ballooned past 300 pounds, tethered to a belief that my worth was measured in physical labor, productivity, and a quiet submission that promised safety. I tied my value directly to my career, my availability, my productivity, and my perceived docility by working, working on a career with little attention to my own needs. The chaos of a childhood marked by survival, a mother battered by violent men, poverty's persistent grip taught me that usefulness was protection and silence was strength. I wrapped myself in perfectionism, worked relentlessly, suppressed my emotions, striving to disprove the cruel words I'd internalized: "You ain't shit, Ashley."

On the surface, it seemed as if I was simply driven, ambitious, and leading with purpose. But beneath the veneer was inherited terror, almost an urgent, aching fear of being seen as lazy, useless, disposable. I wore the mask so well, there were days I forgot it was a mask. I would later come to understand this as an adaptive survival strategy: a trauma-informed capacity to overfunction while staying hidden. What looked like leadership was really the body's brilliance doing whatever it took to stay safe.

Communion: Touched Without Consent

In my late 30s, I shed over 100 pounds, and people noticed. Compliments came in whispers and stares. Hands touched my arms, my back, my stomach without permission. Strangers sat closer, smiled longer, held gazes with a hunger I had known before. That sort of attention was all too familiar, an exposure I'd known before. But this time, it struck with a new kind of terror.

My body was no longer mine alone. It became a canvas for desire, projection, and invasion. I was thrust back into the shadows of my childhood with those buried memories of being sexualized and violated before I even understood safety. The praise for my shrinking BMI was a double-edged sword: a veiled punishment that said, "You're more valuable now. More touchable. More lovable." But to me, it landed like a threat.

Losing weight did not unlock freedom. Instead, it exposed me.

Still, I listen to my body, its rhythms, its right to be seen on my own terms. Not as a performance. Not as fantasy. But as a full, sacred human being, whole and unyielding. My body was telling the truth I had spent years trying to outrun.

Selah: When the Strategy Stops Working

By then, I had frameworks at my fingertips, but I hadn't yet invited them into my body. I knew how to teach transformation but I hadn't yet surrendered to my own. Even my proximity to performing excellence became a hiding place. I remember by 2019, I had been leading leadership work at the intersections of racial equity and self-awareness for a few years. I had the frameworks, knew the tools and crafted beautiful PowerPoint presentations. I moved into leadership roles with a sense of certainty I had worked hard to earn. In one of my early executive positions, I rolled out a strategy that I believed was clean and sharp, backed by data and logic, yet steeped in the human experience of those we were serving, Black and Brown city students and their families. It should have landed. It didn't. The room full of people of color stayed still. Their eyes told me everything, and once again I froze, internally questioning what had happened to my well-coiffed veneer. Why weren't they applauding?

Later that week, my coach didn't criticize the plan. She asked me,

> "What are they hearing and feeling beneath your words?"
> "Are you inviting them in or issuing a command?"

I had spoken with conviction, but lacked connection.

Damn. Pause. That moment, the one where I knew performance without presence wouldn't be enough, never left me. I was gutted. My playbook was failing me. I realized I had built a wall when what they needed was a window. I had led with authority, but not with anchoring in what mattered to them because I was enraptured in nailing the talking points and not talking to the people in front of me. How could I invite them in when I constantly disinvited my own humanity to be present? And beneath it all, I began to feel the cost of the performance I had perfected.

Over time, that moment provided a gateway to a deeper consciousness, a deeper truth: I wasn't afraid of failure. I was afraid of what success might require me to silence: the parts of myself I would have to bury to be accepted. The sound of my own voice disappearing beneath the applause. The presence I was learning wasn't about how I looked on stage. It was about how rooted I felt when no one was clapping.

ALTAR CALL: THE WEEPING BEGINS

Something in me was beginning to unravel, something personal. That fall, I found myself in New Orleans, sitting in a humid ballroom during a Beyond Diversity™ workshop. And I broke down. Not the dignified kind of crying. The kind of wrenching that split me open. The kind that didn't ask for permission, and flowed against my best attempt to hold my emotions at bay. The kind I remember from that cold church floor.

Grief cracked open a door I had kept bolted shut. The pause I had feared became a threshold. That moment was not an ending; it marked a *new* beginning. It was the first time I allowed all of myself … my tenderness, my rage, my joy, my complexity to be witnessed without shame.

True transformation, a shift in "who I be," didn't come all at once. It rippled in waves. It followed through music, therapy, spiritual direction, stillness and internal reckoning. It came through the mirror and through mentors. And it came through reckoning. Not because of a story someone else had shared, but because I finally allowed myself to touch the grief I had been holding on to since childhood. The grief of internalized anti-Blackness. The grief of feeling like I had to earn love. The grief of becoming what the world applauds, and not what my soul was yearning for.

OFFERING: LEADING FROM WITHIN

Today, I choose to practice leading from presence instead of performance. I no longer equate value with volume. I trust silence as much as speech. I believe in the sacredness of pause, of breath, of boundary.

My leadership is not rooted in charisma, although my personality is well and alive. Rather, it is rooted in the courage to be seen. To be disrupted. To be changed.

I walk into rooms carrying all of myself, the hungry child, the masked achiever, the weeping facilitator, the healing man, and I let them speak to one another. That is my integrity. That is my offering. Not the polished speech, but the trembling truth. No applause, just alignment. That is how I lead, now.

I no longer fear being misunderstood. I do fear living a life that is not mine.

So, when I speak now, it is rarely to impress others. It is to remember. It is to remind others that they too can come home to themselves.

BENEDICTION
Benjamin Elijah Mays once said, "The tragedy of life is not found in failure, but in complacency. Not in you doing too much, but doing too little." The line that has stayed with me most is this: "The sin is not in losing, but in low aim."

I have failed. I have fallen. I have lost and I have wept. But I have never aimed low.

Long before I ever stood at a podium or in a pulpit, my mother and others would say I was destined to be a preacher. And while I never took up that call, I have come to understand: I am, without question, a teacher.

And if there is anything my life has taught me, through hunger and hope, through church pews and college halls, through silence and song, it is this: leadership is not something we perform. It is something we live. From within.

So I ask you: Where have you been performing instead of being?

As I return to the mirror, not to perfect or protect the mask, but to meet the man I have become, I ask you: Who are you becoming?

AMEN. AMEN. AMEN.

ABOUT THE AUTHOR

ASHLEY B. STEWART

Ashley B. Stewart (he/him) is an executive coach, facilitator, and advisor who brings intention and heart to every space he enters. As CEO of The Corvian Group, he designs leadership solutions that enhance self-awareness, address unconscious patterns, and foster transformational change. Ashley's facilitation and coaching are grounded in consciousness and a commitment to equity, helping leaders grow with both courage and compassion.

He is a senior leadership advisor at McKinsey & Company and served as the Executive Director of Talent and Organizational Development for Baltimore City Public Schools. His career includes roles at the Annie E. Casey Foundation, Johns Hopkins University, the U.S. Department of State, and the U.S. Department of Education, where he helped launch leadership initiatives for the federal Promise Neighborhoods and Promise Choice grantees and initiatives for the NASA Summer of Excellence and the National Council on Negro Women.

Ashley holds a Bachelor of Arts in psychology from Morehouse College, a Master in Public Policy from Harvard University, a certificate in leadership coaching from Georgetown University, and a Master in Education Leadership from The Broad Center. He is also certified in Courageous Conversations About Race™, Myers-Briggs Type Indicator (MBTI), Emotional Intelligence (EQ-i 2.0), and the Leadership Circle Profile (LCP).

A native of Maryland, Ashley now lives there with his wife and daughters. Whether guiding executive teams or holding space for collective reckoning, he invites leaders into deeper alignment with themselves and their work.

CHAPTER NINE

DYANA LANGLEY-ROBINSON
ROUGH TRUTHS & SMOOTH R&B

If you are still drafting wish lists for Santa or waiting on the Tooth Fairy's Venmo, this chapter might not be for you. If you are here for hard truths and the kind of honesty that makes you flinch and grow, you are in the right place. Let's get into it.

"Not Gon' Cry" – Mary J. Blige

"What do YOU want to be when YOU grow up?" Such vivid memories, not so much of how I would answer the question, but rather my reaction to how other kids would respond.

"You want to be a doctor?"
　　　　"No, thank you!"
"A lawyer?"
　　　　"Not for me."
"A wife and mother?"
　　　　"Maybe, but not a requirement for me."

None of it made much sense until that fortuitous day in the early '90s when my mother took me to her office on Bring Your Daughter to Work Day.

To be honest, I was mostly jazzed to be able to skip school and hang out with my mom. I was thrilled to think we would have an entire day together, just the two of us, and then when my mother added NOT going to school, it was just too perfect. Then, Mom explained we weren't just hanging out all day. We were going to her office and I was going to see what she did at work. I had to remind myself I was "not gon' cry" even if it seemed my day of playing hooky was just a school day in [2]disguise. Of

---

[2] For further details regarding my history of truancy, see my chapter "50 Shades of Gray" in Awareness Put Me On, ed. Chantée Christian (CC Media, 2024), pg. 227–238.

course, my mom couldn't have known at the time how that one day would become such a memorable event in my childhood related to who I am now as a leader. This was when I started answering the question, "Dyana, what do YOU want to be when YOU grow up?" with simply, "A boss!" while remaining blissfully unaware of exactly what that might entail.

Seeing my mother in a totally different role that day planted the seeds for understanding the differences between home and work life and how they intertwine to make us who we are as individuals. All the subsequent experiences and "trials by fire" in my own work life have brought me to a place where I can affirmatively choose and develop my own personal style of leadership centering on authenticity, care, and being a "people-focused" leader. That journey for me, as they all tend to be, started with how I grew up. As an only child of divorced parents, I grew up living in two households that were polar opposites of each other in many ways, yet shared the common ground of unapologetic honesty and truthfulness. It was more than a suggestion in both households; it was simply the way we continued to operate as a family.

When I say unapologetically honest, there were few exceptions. I was that kid in my elementary school who felt the need to debunk inaccuracies such as where babies came from by sharing or conducting anatomically accurate Q&A sessions in the school yard during recess.

"No Maria, it wasn't a stork that dropped off your baby brother. You see, when a woman and a man..."

"Santa? Come on, Julio. That's just your parents pretending. Have you ever seen your parents and Santa in the same room at the same time?"

"Cool that you pulled your tooth out, Tara—but why? You need to realize it's just your parents and now you have put a string around a part of your body, attached it to a door, slammed it shut, and all for a single dollar! Nope. I will wait and let it fall out on its own."

Yes, I was that self-empowered—albeit annoying—classmate wearing

'90s-inspired neon who was responsible for all those reality checks. It never occurred to me that other kids were not getting the same honest and clear truth from their parents.

♫ "Don't Take It Personal (Just One of Dem Days)" – Monica

Before you come for my parents, know that they didn't just dish out honesty to others. I was obsessed with singing as a kid: Whitney Houston on repeat, standing microphone in hand, on a fireplace mantle like it was the Apollo Theatre. No one could tell me I didn't sound just like her. Then one day, driving to school in the back seat of my mother's car, I let out one of my seemingly pitch-perfect Whitney tunes. When I asked my mother how I sounded, she said, and I quote, "You have a very interesting singing voice, dear." In that moment, I felt she might as well have slammed on the car brakes in the same way it felt like she had slammed the brakes on my singing career. Although gutted at the time, I knew my mother was just being honest, and if I had kept believing I could have been the next Toni Braxton, the real world would have been less kind about my singing chops.

Now to this day, my mother insists that "interesting" can also mean distinctively unique, to which I say, "Sure, it does, Ma," but we both know her comment wasn't to be taken "personal" to deter me from ever singing again. What it did do was make me think about my potential strengths and refocus some of my energies into other areas of interest. After the initial shock of questioning my future as the next singing sensation wore off, I began to appreciate my mother's honesty. I remember thinking it was other kids who had it rough. I could take it, so why not be honest? I came to realize at an early age that the honesty of my parents demonstrated respect for my judgment and the choices I made. It helped me to redirect my energies to something more attainable without crushing my dreams or taking away my joy of singing! Rest assured, I continue to joyously sing my heart out daily with one-woman concerts in my car with Whitney, Luther, Alicia—and now my own kids.

My dad's approach was more pragmatic in that he didn't have time or interest in pretending. I remember talking to him about my goals and what I wanted in life. His career advice was pointed and succinct. He would often say, "You were looking for a job when you found this one and you will be looking for a job when you leave this one. Don't take it personally, Pumpkin." I am pretty sure the first time I heard that advice, I was about six.

When I started working and moving into supervisory roles, these foundations factored into my leadership style. I leaned hard into being honest, believing it to be the kindest and most straightforward way of communicating. With the responsibilities of that new role came the added concern of not wanting to lose the relationships I had cultivated with people I valued and admired. As I tried to exert myself in a leadership role, I kept hitting walls with people telling me I was harsh, difficult to work with and even "mean" when it came to providing feedback. It took time, self-reflection, and a few bruises to realize that truth without care can be damaging. I had to learn how my words landed, not just how they were intended. Wasn't that what my parents had taught me to embrace and appreciate?

♪"A House Is Not a Home" – Luther Vandross
Hearing things like "harsh," "militant," "difficult to work with," or even "mean" was shocking. Human Resources asked if I came from a military family and if that was the basis of my leadership style. Although I was not, my father's advice kept playing in my head rent free, reminding me that "business ain't personal, Pumpkin."

Although successful in other areas, I found myself frustrated and confused by the negative feedback. My leadership style clearly did not reflect the level of concern and respect I had for the people around me. Enter my mentor, and the person who took a chance on me when transitioning from my early career in cosmetics to this next chapter in wireless. These are wildly different cultures and communication styles. I told him my concern that if I shared with the team how much I cared about them as individuals, I could appear weak and vulnerable. Another leader might have just moved on or let me flounder, but he spent time with me, sharing his own experiences. He explained that his success as a leader was not attained by focusing solely on pushing people to get what he wanted them to do without also caring for them as individuals. He showed me, by example, that I could be honest and caring in my approach and align it authentically to who I am as a person. My Achilles' heel could be redefined to include my genuine care for the team as individuals without compromising my responsibilities as a leader. This challenge, this pursuit to find and maintain that balance, is ongoing, coupled with the realization that there is no perfect equation. Equally as important is remaining honest with ourselves, which can be the most difficult of all.

As I started to refine what this balance of honesty and care could look like, I noticed almost immediately that my relationships with people, both on my direct teams and across the organization, had changed. People began to open up to me and trust me with parts of their lives that I can't imagine the "militant" version of my leadership style would have embraced. More importantly, they trusted me with both their personal and professional wins and losses. I quickly realized that the door to viewing individuals as whole humans had been opened and was having a positive impact on the functioning and success of the entire team. Anyone could build a house, but I was trying to build a home where people could bring their whole selves and be authentically honest about who they were while still getting the job done effectively.

♪ "How Will I Know?" – Whitney Houston

One team member in particular was struggling to find their way. They were extremely hardworking and yet seemed to be hitting obstacles when it came to both their contribution to the team and success in their career. I decided to take our one-on-one meeting out for lunch. They shared that they weren't "comfortable in their own skin" and were in an unhealthy relationship. They were second-guessing themselves and wondering if they were even in the right job. I took a big deep breath and asked, "Can I be brutally honest without being actually brutal?" They also took a deep breath, and I began to give examples of where I had seen them shine. It wasn't in the current role, but in the "side of desk" activities they were doing; going above and beyond their daily responsibilities. We developed a game plan, maintaining focus on current responsibilities while also defining what success could look like in a role that aligned with their strengths, instead of forcing them into one that did not.

It was important to both of us to crack the code. After being diligent, patient, and open to things that did not fit the mold, opportunities started to come up, highlighting the strengths we had brought to the surface. They landed a lateral role that resulted in making a more positive contribution to the company. Their work and personal lives fell into alignment without the pressures of trying to fit into a work situation that drained them. Although I only carefully danced around the discussion about the personal relationship, taking control of their work life gave them the confidence to make positive changes there as well.

It has been many years since we worked together, but we still keep in touch, and I consider knowing about their continued career and personal life successes to be a great gift. They didn't have to continue giving me a front row seat to their personal story, yet they wanted to acknowledge the positive impact of us both speaking our unapologetic truth and how it changed our viewpoints. I saw how the positive results of this collaborative approach increased my self-awareness and ability to identify personal strengths that would probably not be the AI-suggested version of my LinkedIn profile. It is a simple line that I say today when someone asks me what I am good at: "I love to take teams from good to great." Knowing where and when to take risks and learning from setbacks isn't always pretty, and neither is pushing ourselves out of our comfort zones. I had come to a place in my career where I could take pride in my unpredictable mosaic of acquired skills and experiences that focus on putting the team first. Figuring out how to decode and unlock individual strengths and weaknesses in ways that also had a positive impact on our collective efforts had become my strength and opened a pathway to limitless possibilities that I became excited to explore.

♫"CAN WE TALK?" – TEVIN CAMPBELL

Later in my career, something happened that made me question the strength of these core beliefs. Instead of being the decision-maker, I was the one being pressured to let someone go before working with them long enough to determine what their actual strengths were or if there could be a better role for them. I believed, with more time and care, they could find mutually beneficial success. After all, this is what I had begun to see in myself and hear others describe as one of my leadership strengths: this innate ability to find creative connections in the most unexpected places and people. In this situation, I was under unrelenting pressure from leadership to remove the person from the company. My continued resistance and efforts to find alternatives were not accepted, and I felt myself lose traction, lose my footing in an unfamiliar situation. I will never forget meeting with the person and how they accepted the decision with a level of dignity and grace I had never witnessed under such circumstances. Once all the required information was covered, they then looked me straight in the eye with the most unforgettable strength of character and purpose, in a way that seemed to be concerned about my well-being, and said, "I know this isn't you. I sincerely wish you luck proving your beliefs about being a people-focused leader … but this decision? This isn't you." We had a level of mutual respect and trust, and I knew their comments were made not out of malice or anger, simply an unapologetic truth.

Over the years, I have made similar and difficult decisions. They were my decisions that had been made only after exhausting every other possibility that might change the outcome. Although it was always painful to see someone exit a role this way, I owned those decisions.

The reality of this particular exchange cut so close to my core as a leader that it just about broke me, and if someone who just lost their job could respond with such presence of mind, grace, and honesty, I was determined to follow suit. I can tell myself the fate of this person would have been the same regardless of my continued difference of opinion, but I believe there came a point where I allowed my own sense of vulnerability to determine my truth. Was I rationalizing an action I knew wasn't in line with my beliefs to avoid potentially negative consequences to myself? That is the question I was left with and my response was to never again lose myself to pressures that lead me to make decisions so intrinsically opposite to my core values and ethics. When truth is truth, there is no running away. I do not get to avoid this unfiltered honesty about my own leadership if I am to avoid falling into that space again in the future.

♪ "Ascension (Don't Ever Wonder)" – Maxwell

What is most important to me as I move forward is to lead from within in a way that always challenges the team and myself to be in a better place than where we started. A quote by Maya Angelou has always resonated with me: "I've learned that people will forget what you said, people will forget what you did, but people will never forget how you made them feel." I never want to wonder or have others be uncertain about why I love what I do. Continuing on a path of unapologetic honesty balanced with a sincere caring for individuals will be the legacy I hope to leave, not just as a leader, but as a human.

Although a bit tousled and worse for wear, the dream remains unchanged. I can still smell the air that day back in the 90s when I walked into my mom's office as a young and impressionable kid. I remember her merlot-colored skirt suit, shoulder pads in place with briefcase in hand. I realize now it wasn't about how she looked but how she walked into that office, not just as a leader or a "boss," but as one who seemed to genuinely connect to people with a deep mutual respect. She was kind but firm, and now as an adult, I realize she stood by her values and morals, sometimes at a high cost to herself. I had a front row seat to the times in her career when she chose not to take the path of least resistance, and we all made it through the storm. I know it is possible to ensure that both the outside and inside work selves of the team are authentically considered, and to continually balance the needs of individuals as whole humans against my own responsibilities as a leader.

♪"ALL I DO IS THINK OF YOU" – TROOP

My goal hasn't changed: build teams that defy expectations. This includes being an unapologetically honest leader who doesn't distract or placate with nonexistent bullshit rivaling the myths of Santa or the Tooth Fairy. Learning early in my career that brutal honesty without considering the whole human being can be destructive to the team, it is also true that most people don't wake up in the morning wanting or expecting to fail. People can appreciate hearing the truth about how they can improve and maximize their potential without it being harsh. Part of being a leader is working with individuals to identify those goals and provide the tools and resources to get there and to build up rather than tear down. My responsibility as a leader is to create a respectful and productive environment in which working together results in iron sharpening iron, and superpowers heightening superpowers. It means leading with the heart and mind to constantly refine when and how to apply the tools I have acquired along the way. Ultimately, being an effective and successful "boss" isn't about wielding power or leading through fear. It is about identifying and taking responsibility for how our actions impact others, both individually and collectively, while remaining mindful that we are always a work in progress.

If you are reading this, you weren't dissuaded by my unapologetic honesty about Santa and the Tooth Fairy and you know the standard that I have set for myself to be the "heart first, head always" person I want my children to witness when I take them to my workplace to see what I do (hopefully not in '90s-inspired neon).

♪ **"I'M COMING OUT" – DIANA ROSS**
As a nod to my retail cosmetics days, I offer you this playlist, Rough Truths and Smooth R&B Playlist, as a little "gift with purchase." Go ahead and sing along. I won't judge your "interesting or unique" singing voice.

ABOUT THE AUTHOR

DYANA
LANGLEY-ROBINSON

Dyana Langley-Robinson is a seasoned leader with more than two decades of experience and currently serves as Vice President of Global Talent Development for a major tech company. Her career has been rooted in leading teams, developing leaders, scaling talent strategies, and championing equity and inclusion across global teams.

A first-time bestselling author, Dyana channels her passion for creating opportunity beyond corporate walls by actively supporting organizations that advance access, belonging, and equity for underrepresented communities.

She holds a Master of Business Administration in Marketing from Regis University and a Bachelor of Arts in Mass Communications from the University of Colorado at Denver. She completed the Black Boardroom Initiative program in 2023 and most recently graduated as part of the 2024-2025 cohort of the International Women's Forum (IWF) Fellows Program.

Originally from Denver, Dyana moved to Seattle with her husband, Jeff, in 2015. They have embraced their new city with open arms, finding joy in local coffee shops, bookstores, and wineries, especially during the misty Seattle winters she loves most. Life has become even richer with the arrival of their two children, Liana and Avi, who keep them grounded, laughing, and constantly in awe.

A voracious reader with an overflowing personal library, Dyana finds joy in the little things: a great book, a shared laugh, or an unexpected moment of connection.

PART IV

~

SYSTEMS, LEGACY, & COLLECTIVE CONSCIOUSNESS

"We are ancestors in training. The choices we make today write the stories future generations will inherit."

— Unknown

CHAPTER TEN

DOMINIQUE HOLLINS
TO PLAY OR NOT TO PLAY THE GAME

The American Dream is among history's most enduring scams, a meritocracy myth fueled by propaganda that hard work guarantees success. For too many, it remains a dream deferred. But why? Like many Americans, I internalized that dream. However, as I climbed the ranks of corporate America, I learned a historical truth: access to the dream depends less on merit and more on identity and compliance. The game is falsely advertised as *liberty and justice for all*. Rather, I recognize our institutions as a game of monopoly rigged in favor of dominant groups. While disenfranchised Americans are sold promises of inalienable rights, the wealthy minority manipulate access to those rights. Believing the game is fair is what ensures our compliance. Only when I experienced these truths directly did they become more evident: we are either upholding unjust systems consciously, unconsciously, or stuck in a delusional daze somewhere in the middle. On my journey to becoming a more conscious leader, I experienced a personal transformation. The exhaustion of chasing the "American Dream" triggered a paradigm shift that prompted me to question my level of consciousness, my identity, and my purpose as a global citizen. As you read this chapter, I invite you to reflect on how you've grown to embody conscious leadership.

PLAY THE GAME?

Years ago, I had a manager who was sharp, strategic, and intentional. As one of the few women leaders on our team, I respected how she moved through the workplace. One day, during a one-on-one, we were discussing organizational changes. I comfortably vented and resisted. I didn't realize that she wasn't just asking, she was calculating. She was preparing to expand her territory on the organizational monopoly board and assessing my position. Oblivious, I was taken aback when she interrupted me, elevated her voice, and asked, ***"Dominique, can't*** *you just play the game?!"* Voila! *The game* revealed itself through my leader's moment of frustration. Shocked, I froze. She was offering a growth opportunity had I played by the unspoken rules, but I missed it because I didn't know the rules. I don't remember my response to her, but months later, the organization restructured, I was laid off, and she handed me my walking papers. It was a humbling moment of outrage and activation that heightened my self-awareness. We were playing the same game, but by different rules.

My manager was pursuing wealth and power. I was not. Seeing the disappointment and confusion in her face as she realized I didn't know how to play left me feeling like an imposter. I experienced a deep sense of inadequacy through lack of preparation. I felt like I was caught mismanaging an opportunity and ill prepared for upward mobility. I questioned my talents, abilities, and worth, and I felt betrayed and naive. It was a tough pill to swallow, but it was necessary for deeper self-reflection. That experience left me asking: *If the game is already rigged, what does it mean to truly play and win on my own terms?* I needed to better examine my position as a player.

Growing up, I despised the board game *Monopoly*. I remember many game nights spent fighting over fake land and fake power that always ended the same way: a few winners, many losers. Ironically, Elizabeth Magie invented *Monopoly* in 1902 (then called *The Landlord's Game*) to illustrate the dangers of monopolies! I didn't realize I was a piece in America's real-life version. I thought I understood the game. But the truth was: no one taught me how to play by its unwritten rules. I learned that knowing how to play by these rules is a form of privilege. I believed merit would be enough. My manager knew better. Whether or not I wanted to play, the game was playing me. I needed a different strategy, but I needed to better understand the game first. This awakening pushed me to study the history of corporate power and how it mirrors our national politics.

THE MONOPOLY OF CORPORATE AMERICA

For years, I've advocated for diversity, equity, inclusion, and accessibility (DEIA) and its relationship to the workplace and American politics. Like those before me, I warned, if we were not mindful of the lessons (and reasoning) of history that we were bound to repeat them. Unfortunately, too many people believed that our country was so far along the path of equal rights that we wouldn't possibly go back to the 1960s. To some, I appeared to be a fearmonger. Now, under the 47th presidential administration, history has returned with a vengeance. In just 6 months, federal cuts to key resources in healthcare, education, and workplace equity have disproportionate impacts on America's most vulnerable citizens. Close behind is a long list of corporations that quickly supported these policies. Some corporations, like Target, faced a $12.4 billion backlash after dismantling its DEI programs. This is just one example of why it is important that we recognize corporate America as both a byproduct and contributor to the legislative woes that we're facing as a country.

From   2008 corporate bailouts to unqualified tech CEOs being commissioned as senior officers in the military in 2025, we see how corporate influence and entitlement flourishes as civilian welfare diminishes. Darwinistic survival practices overrule basic human rights in favor of dominant social groups. From HR cover-ups to executive disputes, I've witnessed how leaders prioritized power over people. Conformity is rewarded, causing new employees to quickly adopt toxic behaviors in hopes of acceptance and promotion. I was one of those unwitting employees focused more on output than collaboration. Driven by a mechanistic worldview that treats people like objects rather than human beings, corporate America is American politics in business. Whether we're highlighting the disproportionate representation of Fortune 500 CEOs, healthcare disparities, homelessness, joblessness, or a disappearing middle class, the lack of fairness across American institutions reflects bias woven into the tapestry of American identity. If we're not aware of these parallels, then we're more likely to perpetuate them.

For most of my life, I avoided seeing these truths because it would require me to do something about it—what could I do about it? *Playing the game translates to "uphold the monopoly of structural inequity."* Afraid and unsure, I complied, like millions of Americans yet to be awakened. Now, I'm using my voice to share what I've learned in hopes of being a mirror to others. My workplace experiences taught me valuable lessons about the importance of self-awareness and history. This knowledge helped me develop a more informed worldview which birthed pathways towards my *why*.

DEFINING YOUR "WHY"

While systemic inequities play out in corporate and political arenas, the impact is deeply personal. I learned this firsthand. Shortly after my "play the game" experience, I found myself disillusioned in a role where I believed I could affect real change. Recruited under the impression that leadership was committed to cultural development, I quickly realized my position was more performative than substantive. During my interview, my manager's attempt to connect with a dance move signaled subtle tokenization, but I ignored it at the time. Once in the role, I learned of employee experiences and leadership decisions that contradicted the values the organization claimed to uphold. Lesson learned: while playing the game, pay attention to the signs; your intuition is rarely wrong. I began to understand the limitations of my role, as more signs revealed themselves to me.

During a one-on-one strategy meeting, my manager called me *inspiring* and said I represented *hope* for the company. I became incensed. While I understood the importance of what she was conveying, I didn't want to be tokenized as a symbol for progress. I didn't want to be viewed as an *Uncle Tom*, upholding the values of oppressive systems that hurt me and my community. My anger revealed how far this role was from my personal values and belief systems. My chest deflated, I exhaled slowly, and I could feel the warmth of the blood coursing through my veins. I was evolving. I asked myself, *Why am I here? To be a part of the change or to represent the idea of change?* I reminded myself to **be the change,** a key message in an article that I wrote and published while at the company. After six months, I resigned from my position and redirected my time and energy to increase my investments in my business, advocating more intentionally and authentically.

Leaving was tough, but my integrity mattered more than my salary or status. It was another reminder of how other players in the game are operating and how it can impact my strategy. My manager and I had two different strategies for navigating this organization's systems. She was focused on her ambitions and it was my responsibility to advocate for my own. My decision to leave was a conscious one, rooted in self-awareness and reconnection to my personal *why*. These decisions are not always easy and sometimes come with great sacrifices, which in the long run prove to be worth it. While I was proud of having acquired the job, I was also proud that I chose my integrity in the end. My *why* was more important than my circumstances. It also shined light on the depths of my identity—who am I in relation to my *why*?

IDENTITY, POWER, & PRIVILEGE

I used to believe in meritocracy. My first job in tech taught me otherwise. My intellect and achievements did not matter in the face of bias, microaggressions, and a lack of support in an environment of elitism, entitlement, and inequity. Like many people, DEIA only became important to me when it affected my life directly. Faced with the discomfort of personal injustice, avoidance and denial were no longer an option. I was forced to choose a side and I became a change agent, using my privilege to advocate for my rights and others. I had no idea how this decision would change my career journey.

The challenges in my first job helped me leverage my background as a business analyst, operator, and communicator to champion workplace justice. I began in employee resource groups (ERGs), creating visibility for and amplifying the voices of underrepresented people. In time, I spoke on stages, led programs, and became an executive DEIA consultant. One day, I participated on a panel of tech leaders, sharing our insights on the value of DEIA in the industry. Attendees often appreciated that I spoke candidly and in relatable ways which attendees appreciated most. I used my voice as an empowerment tool for myself and others. A chocolate-skinned Black woman approached me and asked, *"Have you considered your complexion is why you can speak so freely?"* As a light-skinned Black woman, I was shaken. I wanted to defend myself by recounting everything I'd endured. I understood the troubled history of colorism, and yet I'd never considered how it had benefited me.

I recounted the many ways colorism showed up in my family dynamics as well as the broader Black community, causing generational fissures across the African diaspora. With this in mind, I gathered myself and responded humbly by saying, *"You know what? You're right. No, I've actually never thought about that. Thank you for bringing this aspect of privilege to my awareness. While I believe I'm speaking from a place of truth, I never considered who is 'allowed' to speak and who may not feel that same safety."* Quietly we stood in the awkward moments that followed. Cocooned in a precious silence while surrounded by the noise of the crowd, our eyes met once more as if to exchange a powerful moment in our shared history: she spoke her piece on my colorism privilege, and I understood my responsibility as a beneficiary of that privilege. Yes, we were both players in the game with many shared attributes, but I still had an advantage. We parted ways, but that moment created another pivotal identity shift within me.

Afterwards, I noticed colorism everywhere and I became more aware of my privilege. I thought, *If I was oblivious about the privilege of my skin color in an anti-Black society, then what other privileges did I carry that I was unaware of?* I began reflecting on how layers of my identity, both marginalized and privileged, shaped my experience. I was so focused on advocating for my rights as a queer Black woman that I overlooked the many privileges I also carried. I wondered, *Am I unintentionally perpetuating the systems I'm fighting against?* It is difficult to see someone else's oppression if we're only focused on our own. In light of this, I changed my business practices, leaning into self-reflection as a primary tool for systems change. Conscious leadership, I learned, isn't just about dismantling external systems. It begins with an unflinching look at ourselves. I decided to lean into my privilege and use it to my advantage with intention, which is the very task I'd been asking of the dominant majority!

ANALYZING THE GAME

Since 2010, I've guided individuals, teams, and organizations through DEIA strategy and integration. From boardrooms to casual conversations, I've seen how identity, privilege, and perspective shape our understanding of equity. Sometimes, these conversations offered pathways towards connection and other times they served as mirrors, reflecting underlying beliefs and values. I've discovered that our stories reveal the same truth: the social injustice problems we face in the workplace aren't just structural. They're spiritual. Something is broken in the human spirit, a fracture so deep that it convinces us to harm, exclude, and devalue one another as if we are not all connected. From science to spirituality to culture, there is ample evidence to support our interconnectedness as a species. While I never imagined my career journey would lead me on a journey towards consciousness, learning DEIA as I practiced with others helped to expand my consciousness. From evaluating myself, to my relationships, to oppressive systems, to the underlying conditions that led us here, I discovered that capitalism is a symptom of spiritual disconnection.

Before I was programmed into an American illusion, I had goals, dreams, and unlimited creativity. I underwent great lengths to decolonize my worldview, shifting from a mechanistic (objectification) to a humanistic view (mutual respect). From psychotherapy to Ayahuasca ceremonies, my personal transformation journey included decades of therapy, spiritual practices, and consciousness studies. *The game* was not only causing anguish in my mind, but also my heart and body. Psychotherapy was a start towards self-discovery, but alone it was insufficient. When therapy didn't work, I turned to prayer. In December 2021, I dropped to my knees and prayed for spiritual restoration. Since then, my prayers have been answered through international travel, spiritual encounters, and major life changes. I wanted to give up on myself, but the process of reclamation helped me to endure. This is a testimony in faith, endurance, and determination.

MAKING THE DECISION

My journey has answered a lifetime of questions. Chief among them: *what is wrong with humanity*? DEIA led me to a much deeper insight: disconnection from our collective consciousness makes us vulnerable to division. The mechanistic worldview that governs us is rooted in power, separation, and commodification. We've strayed from indigenous models of interdependence, shared prosperity, and reverence for nature in place of industrialization, normative dissociation, and greed. This transition to capitalistic individualism instead of collective economics has led us to a divisive monopoly.

I've felt this divisiveness since I was a child and now I understand why. It's intentional. *Playing the game causes us to fight for resources.* The solution is in our collective pursuit of *liberty and justice for all.* My consciousness journey brought me new understanding. Now, I'm dedicated to awakening as many of us as I can, using my skills and talents. My new path is heart-centered local community events, centering marginalized small business owners. This is a 180-degree pivot from my sole obsession of personal wealth building and capitalistic gain. One solution I've developed is Mosaic Moments, a service that offers community experiences, centering culture, cuisine, and connection. Participants are essential components of the mosaic experience, producing dynamic opportunities for collaboration. Rather than centering corporations, this solution focuses on empowering people directly, using the skills I learned while *playing the game.*

Throughout this chapter, I've shared stories to help you see yourself more clearly through my vulnerability as an individual, during interpersonal encounters, and in the ways that I navigate oppressive systems. I've grown to believe we are more connected than we understand, but we have to condition ourselves to look beyond our own perspectives to see the connections we share with others. Have you recognized yourself in any of these moments? Are you playing the game? How did you learn how to play? Our personal awakening often follows an internal crisis of ego or identity, but it also unlocks the opportunity for clarity. The pursuit of conscious leadership begins with knowing who you are and how that shapes your worldview. I learned concretely that change must begin *within* us before change can take place *through us.*

An identity crisis prompted me to seek truth about my concept of reality. My journey continues, but I am much further along than before. Rumi said, "What you seek is seeking you." So ask yourself: *What do I understand about the American game of monopoly? What kind of player am I in this game? What's my "why"? What's my plan?* If you find yourself struggling to answer these questions, then reach out to me or others in your community who are further along in their conscious leadership journey. Maybe we can explore together. Whether this journey is prompted by a personal crisis, your workplace, family, community, or otherwise, it must begin with a more conscious version of you. The choice is yours: will you continue to play the game or will you help us change it?

Dynamics of Conscious Leadership

WE360

REFLECT – LOOK INTO THE MIRROR:
Individual – Consciousness
1. When was the last time I listened to my inner voice—even when it disrupted the status quo?
2. What beliefs or stories have I inherited that no longer serve me as a leader?
3. What does "truth" feel like in my body, and how do I know when I'm suppressing it?

Interpersonal – DEIA as Practice
1. How do I show up in conversations where difference or discomfort is present?
2. What assumptions am I making about others based on their identities or roles?
3. Who in my life helps me expand my understanding of inclusion and who might I be overlooking?

Systemic – Culture as a Mirror
1. What unspoken rules exist in my organization—and who do they bene fit or harm?
2. How am I complicit in maintaining systems that exclude, and how can I shift that?
3. What would a truly inclusive, conscious culture look like in my world—and what's one step I can take toward it?

Spiritual – Awakening to Wholeness
1. What parts of myself have I silenced or ignored in order to succeed, and what might happen if I allowed them to speak?
2. How do I currently connect with something greater than myself— whether through faith, nature, community, or creativity and how does that shape my leadership?
3. In what ways is my spirit calling me to expand beyond survival and step into a life of deeper authenticity and service?

ABOUT THE AUTHOR

DOMINIQUE
M. HOLLINS

Dominique M. Hollins is a strategic business and operations leader with nearly two decades of experience driving inclusive transformation across the tech, SaaS, and Fortune 500 sectors. Her expertise spans executive coaching, process optimization, client success, and scalable program design—delivering impactful results for companies such as eBay, Google, and Hone HQ.

As founder and CEO of WĒ360, Dominique has advised over thirty global organizations, helping them embed equity into HR systems, enhance employee experience, and align business operations with inclusive leadership values. She is widely recognized for bridging strategy and execution to create lasting change in complex, fast-paced environments.

Dominique is currently pursuing a master's degree in consciousness, psychology, and transformational studies. Her graduate work deepens her understanding of the human mind, emotional intelligence, and spiritual development as they manifest in individuals, relationships, and systems. These studies inform her healing-centered, holistic approach to leadership and community empowerment.

She brings this integrative perspective to her role as a board member of The T.R.U.T.H. Project in Texas, where she is committed to advancing the emotional and cultural wellness of LGBTQIA+ communities of color through creative arts and transformative dialogue.

A sought-after speaker and facilitator, Dominique is known for her authenticity, vision, and unwavering commitment to equity, belonging, and collective healing. When she is not working, you can find her traveling, spending time in nature, enjoying a great meal, or designing immersive cross-cultural experiences.

CHAPTER ELEVEN

JAMES T. HARRIS

FROM LEGACY TO LEADERSHIP: LESSONS MY FATHER NEVER SPOKE, BUT ALWAYS LIVED

"I didn't realize I was learning to lead; I just thought I was watching my dad be my dad." — James T. Harris

He never sat me down with a manual. He didn't need to. His life was the lesson. The way he treated people. The way he showed up: disciplined, reliable, and steady, even when life wasn't. As a kid, I didn't have the language for it, but I felt it. And later, as I walked into rooms where I was the only one who looked like me, I inherited his leadership style. His example taught me that leadership isn't always loud. Sometimes it looks like quiet confidence, choosing to listen

Young James and his father eating popsicles.

more than you speak, or knowing when to speak up even when it costs you something. This chapter is my reflection on that kind of leadership, the kind that grows from within, shaped by love, legacy, and lived experience.

I DIDN'T THINK MY DAD LOVED ME UNTIL HE CRIED ON MY SHOULDER. I love my dad. I want to establish that strongly upfront. The more I live, the more I understand him and the reality that the role of father, husband, head of household, or simply adult does not come with a playbook. We do what we know. We emulate what we see. My dad did all he knew to do at that time in his life. He provided. My mother and father worked tirelessly to provide for me and my brother. Like many men, my father believed his sole value came from his ability to provide for his family, and because of that, we did not lack much. What I lacked was affection from my father.

"I CAN COUNT ON ONE HAND THE NUMBER OF TIMES MY FATHER TOLD ME HE LOVED ME."

My father and I have a similar story. He grew up with his siblings in a two-parent household with a father who was, for lack of a better word, tough. More specifically, tough on him. My grandfather, my namesake, James Harris by most accounts, was a hard man; partly due to the time in history in which he was raising a family, partly due to many dreams deferred, and partly due to his chosen vices. He passed away when I was five years old. I choose to believe he did the best he could with the tools he had. Throughout the years, my father and I have had many discussions about my upbringing (thanks to a lot of therapy on my part) and he often responds the same way: "I wasn't perfect, but I tried to be better than my father. I can count on one hand the number of times my father told me he loved me." My dad lacked affection from his father, too.

There is an unintentional compounding effect when a man who was deprived of affection is then tasked with raising a son. In my case, the inability to show love came in the form of harsh discipline and strict parenting. He was in the Reserve Officers' Training Corps (ROTC) as a child, and we were often in our own form of basic training. There weren't a lot of discussions in the household, just orders that we all had to adhere to immediately. The opening of the garage that signaled he was home sent a wave of anxiety throughout the house as we scrambled to make sure everything was clean before he came in to inspect. A cluttered living room or unmade bed would pave the way for anger and hurtful conversations. When I was in high school, I had a speech and debate tournament coming up, a big one. I'd been winning, and I wanted my dad to see me in my element. I waited until he came home on Friday, building up the courage all afternoon. The garage door opened, that familiar clatter of metal, followed by his heavy steps into the kitchen. My heart raced, equal parts excitement and anxiety.

"Hey Dad, are you coming to my tournament this weekend?" I asked. He barely looked up. "HELL NO."

The words landed like a punch. My chest tightened, and the warmth in my face wasn't pride, it was humiliation. I never asked him again.

At the time, I told myself I must not be worth the time. But years later, I realized that moment shaped my leadership philosophy more than almost any other. I vowed that no one—my wife, my kids, my team—would ever feel that same dismissal in my presence. In my career, I've leaned toward a human-first leadership style, one where people feel seen and heard, even when I can't give them the answer they want. That commitment was born in my kitchen that Friday night. That day also planted the seed for another core belief of mine: that not every moment of leadership is easy or uplifting, but each moment matters if it moves people forward with dignity. That moment also reinforced what my father always said about work: it's not supposed to be glamorous all the time. Work is work, and showing up with consistency is part of earning trust as a leader.

That feeling of anxiety when "the boss" was around was one I didn't want anyone to have around me, whether it was my wife and kids, or those I worked with. Not wanting others to feel that way around me has influenced the nurturing approach I take with my sons and the human-first approach I take with the teams that I lead. I've often overindexed on this though, and have worked to find a balance between nurturing and holding others accountable.

There was a stark difference between the person we experienced at home and the person who showed up in my father's career. The lack of patience he had with me at home showed up in abundance for those who worked for him. My dad is a born leader and admired by those he has worked for, worked with, and by those who have worked for him. There is a special feeling you get when a leader pours into you and your career; when someone in a higher position than you acknowledges you, sees you. My father, throughout his 40-plus-year career as a civil engineer, was amazing at that. I was always amazed at how he made people feel, how they were so willing to work hard for him, and how much they respected him. I decided at an early age that regardless of the field I went into, I would learn how to make people feel the way my father did at work.

EXCELLENCE WITH CARING ON THE HIGHEST OF SEVEN HILLS

I attended Florida Agricultural and Mechanical University (FAMU), the best HBCU in the land, drawn by its School of Business and Industry (SBI), the influence of close friends, and the example my father set by leaving home to pursue education. Moving to Tallahassee felt like stepping into a new world, one where I would discover who I was.

FAMU was more than academics. It was an incubator for self-reflection, resilience, and leadership. At SBI, we led student-run companies that kept the school running, offering a safe environment to practice decision-making and accountability. I quickly stepped into leadership roles, leaning on my father's example of discipline, fairness, and care for people.

During this time, something unexpected began to happen; my dad and I started to have real conversations. I missed home, I missed my mom and my family, and I called… a lot. And this was before free long distance—this was calling on calling cards, and nighttime minutes, and a lot of daytime minutes that were not free. I recognize this sounds crazy to some and I'm dating myself, but believe it or not, there was a time when cell phones had a set number of minutes you could talk on for free during the day (before 6 or 7 p.m.) and many plans had unlimited "night time" minutes (after 6 or 7 p.m.). If you didn't have a cell phone, you used a calling card. What I'm saying is these calls weren't free, and I was making them often. Initially, I called to talk to my mom and my brother, but there was a voice in the background saying "Tell him…" followed by lessons and nuggets that only a father could give. Eventually, instead of speaking through relayed messages from my mom and brother, my dad would grab the phone to speak directly to me. At first, our conversations were clumsy, like two people learning a new language. But over time, they became a lifeline.

One night, I was stressing about a leadership decision for a student-led company in the SBI, whether to give harsh feedback to someone working on a project. My dad said, "Son, it's not about being liked—it's about being respected for doing what's right." The next day, I made the call. It wasn't easy, but it was fair. That was my first real taste of leadership, the kind rooted in accountability, not popularity, and it came directly from those long-distance calls. Those conversations also taught me that hard work, especially the unglamorous kind, builds trust and credibility over time. Those conversations also taught me an important truth I still share with young professionals: sometimes you have to do what you have to do, to do what you want to do. The grind, the late nights, the uncomfortable roles, they position you for the opportunities you've been dreaming about.

What I found through these conversations with my dad was profound and at the same time incredibly simple. He did his best. He did what he knew. And most importantly, the man that I saw as Superman was indeed just a man, like me, trying to figure out this thing called life. There was something freeing in that realization. That realization unlocked more than the connection between my father and me; it began to unlock something within me. I began to connect the dots between my father's conversations and leadership and the lessons of leadership that he showed me through his actions, to the way that I was instinctively living my life. Sometimes you are learning things without knowing you are being taught. Langston Hughes penned:

> *"And the lectures you deliver may be very fine and true*
> *But I'd rather get my lesson by observing what you do.*
> *For I may misunderstand you and the fine advice you give,*
> *But there's no misunderstanding how you act and how you*
> *live." (from "Live Your Creed" by Langston Hughes)*

By my father living his creed daily, I knew what it took to lead and take responsibility. When bonds for transportation projects passed, he gave credit to the team. When they failed, he faced the board himself. I didn't just hear about accountability—I watched it.

Years later, I found myself in a similar position at work. My team had missed a critical hiring deadline for a major product launch. I could have pointed fingers. Instead, I stepped into the meeting and owned it: "This one's on me. Here's how we'll fix it." My team later told me that moment built their trust more than any success we'd shared. That wasn't an accident. It was the same lesson I learned watching my father walk into those board meetings—steady, responsible, and unflinching. It was a reminder that the last stretch of a challenge is often the toughest, and it's in that moment that leaders earn respect by finishing strong. Watching him navigate those moments taught me that hard work beats talent in the long run, because discipline and perseverance are what carry you across the finish line. And when you're in the final stretch, that last 5%, it's often the hardest part, but it's where true leaders set themselves apart.

"But…it's still the South!"

When it came time to decide where I would go after graduation, I chose Atlanta, GA, because I thought that's where I needed to be. Leaving home (California at the time) to move to Atlanta was difficult, but I believed it to be what I needed to do at the time, and because my father had moved quite a bit throughout his career and lived away from family, I figured he would understand. To my surprise, the day I left for the airport, he grabbed my shoulder, looked me in the eye, and told me to be safe. I reassured him that I had been living on my own for years during college. He grabbed me, hugged me close, put his head on my shoulder, and cried, "But it's still the South and you are my son." Until this point in my life, I could only remember my father expressing a few emotions towards me: a small amount of happiness and a lot of anger. I had never seen him cry openly. I grew up feeling rejected by him, which caused resentment towards those who had a relationship with him. I longed for the love of a father and was lonely without it. In that moment, he showed the love he had toward me. It was as if a weight was being lifted off my shoulders, and the feelings of self-doubt, loneliness, and worthlessness that I had been carrying for years began to fade. I know now that my dad has always loved me in the ways he knew how, but, in that moment, in the hallway leading to the garage, as I prepared to start my adult life, I knew he loved me.

"I hope you got something from me…"

My dad and I have had countless conversations about life, some light, some hard, but all rooted in love and a desire to understand each other as men. More than once, he's said, "Well, I hope you got something from me while you were coming up." The truth is: I got everything from him. The man I am today exists because of the lessons he taught me, sometimes in words, often in silence.

If I could speak to that boy who mistook quiet for a lack of love, I'd tell him: *Hold on. Watch closely. The lessons are in the long drives, the hard conversations, and the example set when no one is watching.* I'd tell him that love shows up in different ways and that no one is perfect, but he has always been loved.

My dad never handed me a leadership manual. He gave me something better: living proof that leadership isn't about titles or applause. It's about showing up, doing the work, and carrying others with you. I am the leader I am today not despite his flaws, but because of how he kept showing up anyway. That's the Harris legacy, rooted in valuing every person, from the most junior to the most senior, and leading with both strength and humanity. And it's sustained by knowing that everyone matters and that peace, whether found in family, travel, or a quiet golf course, keeps a leader going for the long haul.

James and dad at FAMU graduation.

I carry that legacy forward every time I choose to lead in the way he taught me: with consistency, respect, and heart.

Thanks, Dad.

ABOUT THE
AUTHOR

JAMES
HARRIS

James Harris is a dynamic talent executive, inclusion strategist, and entrepreneur with nearly two decades of experience leading transformative recruiting initiatives in the tech industry. As director of talent acquisition at a major tech company, he oversees high-performing, globally distributed teams and drives inclusive hiring strategies that help shape the future of work.

A proud Rattler and graduate of Florida A&M University, James has a background in competitive speech and debate and blends strategic thinking with the power of storytelling—whether in the boardroom or on stage. He is an emerging voice in the professional speaking world, known for his insights on leadership, equity, and legacy-building. Passionate about empowering professionals, he helps others build generational wealth, grow in their purpose, and lead with authenticity.

James is a devoted husband and father of two young sons, and lives by the principle that success is measured not only by income, but by the impact you leave behind. Whether leading teams, negotiating deals, or influencing employment and inclusion practices, James brings vision, integrity, and hustle to every endeavor.

He currently lives in Celina, Texas, with his wife and two sons. When he is not fighting the good fight, you can find James (trying) to golf, coaching youth basketball, or keeping his son's fingers out of electrical sockets.

CHAPTER TWELVE

CHANTÉE L. CHRISTIAN
AND SUDDENLY...SHIFT HAPPENS

"You either walk inside your story and own it, or you stand outside your story and hustle for your worthiness." —Brené Brown

Countless times, people have told me they wish they had my life or aspire to be like me. If I had a dollar for every time, I'd be a trillionaire. I make a conscious effort to correct them in the moment because, let's be honest, I've painted a pretty picture of my life on social media, but that's not the whole truth. What they don't see are the messy parts, the duct tape holding things together, the prayers that feel unanswered, the mascara running down my face.

Leadership isn't perfect. It's faith practiced out loud. It's holding on through the chaos, bucking up for the ride, and still showing up anyway. Most days I barely have time to buckle up before the ride starts. And just like any other rollercoaster, I hang on and keep my hands inside. So I invite you to buckle up with me as you read because this ride isn't polished or perfect.

As unbelievable as it may seem, I'm human, too. Remember that song "Superwoman" by Alicia Keys? Sometimes I have to sing it to myself. I'm not just preaching—I'm taking my own advice. This chapter is me showing you what it looks like to practice walking in faith out loud.

So, if you catch glimpses of duct tape, contradictions, or me hollering like I'm on a rollercoaster—it's not by accident. That's leadership to me: raw, resilient, still moving forward. Leadership isn't perfection, it's presence. It's showing up anyway.

The reason I can seemingly hold it together has nothing to do with perfection, and everything to do with God, coaching, therapy, bourbon, whiskey, and an unmatched network of people around me. More recently, I'm making conscious efforts to share more of the messy because entrepreneurship is not all wins and highlight reels.

Public Service Announcement

Allow me to reintroduce myself…my name is Chantée L. Christian (go back and read that like HOV said it in "Public Service Announcement"). I am not here to sell you perfection. I am here to share with you my truth. I am living proof that leadership is not about having it all together. It's about showing up while the screws are still loose, the duct tape is visible, and the tears from seemingly unanswered prayers are still wet. It's about moving anyway, because I know there are people who won't move until I do.

Back in 2020/2021, when I co-authored my first bestseller *Leading Through the Pandemic*, I thought I was giving you all a snapshot of who I was becoming. What I didn't know then (and know too well now) is that the becoming never stops. Just when I think I've figured it out, life clears its throat and says, "Nah, sis… you're getting a little too cozy."

If you're looking for a polished package tied with a cute ribbon, this is not the chapter for you. Think of our time together as *show and tell*.

I'd be remiss not to mention that I'm a Christian, squared. Yep—double the dose. My last name is Christian, and I'm also a Christian. Go ahead, let it sink in. That joke never gets old for me. You didn't laugh? That's okay—I laughed enough for both of us.

Here's the biggest disclaimer of them all: you're going to hear me talk to God like we're friends because in my mind, we are. Some people might clutch their pearls over that. Sorry, not sorry. This chapter isn't about theology or your interpretation of it. It's about me—my perspective, my journey.

And no, I'm not everybody's cup of tea. That's cool. Because I'm someone's shot of whiskey—strong, a little fiery, and not for the faint of heart. Like the great prophetess Erykah Badu once said, *"I'm an artist, and I'm sensitive about my shit!"* So tread lightly with your critiques. I'm still a work in progress. God isn't done with me yet.

Alright. Now that the preliminaries are out of the way—let's get into it.

EVERYTHING THAT GLITTERS AIN'T GOLD
I joke often that if I put as much effort into myself as I've put into other people's children—by "children" I mean these women's dusty ass sons (*insert a true-to-form Chantée eye roll*)—I'd be unstoppable. Funny, yes. Also painfully true. The most intimate relationship any of us will ever have is the one we have with ourselves. And yet, it's the one we neglect the most.

Because the truth is: we pour so much energy into chasing, keeping, and fixing—partners, clients, jobs, careers, ideas, concepts—you name it. We'll be the biggest cheerleaders and advocates for everyone except for ourselves. We tell ourselves leadership is all about pushing others forward, when in reality, it starts with pulling ourselves into alignment.

Think about how much energy we spend trying to be seen, liked, or considered. We can say "IDGAF" all day, but the truth is we do. We're built to care. That's part of why social media is so powerful—it exposes both our securities and insecurities, and it lures us into comparison. Most people would argue that comparison is a trap. I'd argue that if you allow it to push you into action, it's doing exactly what it's supposed to. Providing you with motivation to get what your heart desires.

I like to think of social media like a Pinterest board (I don't know how this line will age, lol). For me, it's a collection of things I desire, ideas I think, people I admire, and the energy I want to exemplify. People laugh when I say I build my "For You" page brick by brick, but I do. I curate the experiences I want. And it's a constant reminder for me to pay attention to what I give my energy to.

So here's my confession—the first of many, I'm sure: I haven't always been fully obedient to what I know I'm called to do. Sure, I've been obedient. You've seen the fruits of it—coaching, mentorship, launching a multimedia arm of my business, stepping onto stages, and more. But God has also told me to create a coaching program that I'm holding hostage in my drafts because of partial obedience. OR I'll have a great idea to post on social media, but won't because it isn't perfect.

Somewhere between the yes and the follow-through, I've let doubt, ego, inconvenience, or frustration creep in. Sound familiar? Sitting on something you need to release into the world? Imagine if you leaned into full obedience and released it.

> *"The place where you are broken is the place where light can break through."* (adapted from the wisdom of Leonard Cohen and Rumi)

PRAYED FOR IT, PAID FOR IT

Back in the early 2000s, I was an adjunct faculty member at Prince George's Community College (PGCC), which led me to teach at George Mason University (Mason) in 2019. I had been itching to get back into the classroom. I love seeing students connect the dots and go on to achieve things they hadn't dreamt of or thought were possible. So when I finally landed an adjunct position in the Communication Department at Mason, it felt like an answered prayer.

Until the first day of class.

I sat in traffic for a little over two hours—on a commute that should've taken 30 minutes. Somewhere around the one-hour mark, that answered prayer started feeling like punishment. There I was, questioning my life choices and quickly forgetting that this was the very thing I had been on God's line about. Aka...I had been begging and praying for it.

The irony wasn't lost on me. I had asked for this opportunity. And because the package didn't look and feel like I wanted it to, I was treating it like a burden instead of a blessing. That, my friends, is what partial obedience looks like—accepting the assignment, and complaining about the perceived inconvenience.

In that moment, I had to shift my posture—literally and metaphorically. I adjusted in my seat, switched off the hype music, and reminded myself of two things: I prayed for this. And faith is publicly walking the prayers I once whispered in private.
Even when traffic is hell on wheels. Even when the answer doesn't come packaged in red bottoms or applause. It indeed is still an answered prayer.

I'm curious: what have you been asking/begging for, only to find yourself complaining once you receive it?

PUSH IT TO THE LIMIT
They say all hell breaks loose right before a breakthrough; and I can testify to that. Society has sold us this idea that breakthroughs are magical, fireworks-in-the-sky moments. The truth? Most breakthroughs show up as breakdowns.

Picture it… Columbia, South Carolina, 2006. A young Chantée, barely 23, living the good life—or so I thought. And then BOOM! Just like that, I was in the hospital. Have you ever gone to the emergency room and they immediately took you back? Well, I have. And, I can guarantee you it is not a good sign. So, of course, I was convinced I was dying. My head had been pounding for days. I came home from work, sat on the couch, and blacked out. Next thing I know, I'm hooked up to IVs—ice pack on my head, negotiating, bargaining with God not to let my parents have to bury me (their only egg).

The tests showed I had severe, stress-induced migraines. I had been running on fumes, pushing past every limit, wearing my grind like a badge of honor. Those migraines weren't random—they were my body's protest, my spirit's smoke alarm. My breakthrough was realizing I couldn't keep glorifying my grind. Hustle had me hollow. Leadership didn't mean proving I could run on empty. It meant choosing rest as a radical act.

And let me tell you, breakdowns don't stop at hospitals. They show up in other ways, too. There is this post floating around social media about being "9-to-5 broke" versus "entrepreneur broke." The creator says that when you're "9-to-5 broke," you're just waiting on the next payday. And when you're "entrepreneur broke," you're waiting on the next client, the next deal, the next miracle. Hit different it does! It is one of the most humbling experiences you'll encounter, to decide between gas and groceries, the doctor or the hair salon. And before you judge or call that vanity, remember that my appearance is part of how I get paid. So for me, those choices carry a lot of weight.

I even drove for Amazon Flex for a while—yes, me, delivering packages. For anyone who doesn't know, some Amazon deliveries are done by independent drivers. I was sure God had left me. I remember riding around feeling like Moses in the wilderness, yelling, "God, where are you? Do you even hear me? Uhhhh, sir?! How did I get here?"

I was a mess! It had me singing like Anthony Hamilton: "I'm a mess right now…Bills are piling high…Like living in a blender, I'm shaken, and I'm stirred." Through the tears, prayers, complaining (mostly to myself), hauling bags of cat and dog food twice my size, one thing became extremely clear to me…I was wasting my gift and not walking in my purpose. God didn't tell me to go work for Amazon Flex; I thought it would help me. Truth be told, I was being disobedient, trying to fix my problems my way instead of doing the thing He'd asked me to do. And I had the nerve to be begging for Him to "show up like only you can." Truth be told, I wouldn't have answered me either…

Gracefully Broken

In the midst of it all came what felt like heartbreak after heartbreak. Navigating the intersections of grief and happiness (not joy, happiness), I thought I was doing okay. And then came heartbreak in its most devastating form. My friend, fellow Aquarian, and co-author of *Awareness Put Me On*, Nikki, passed away unexpectedly. Losing her left me feeling hollow. She was a light, and when "the light" went out, I wrestled with the grief that felt like emotional quicksand. I still had to keep showing up for others, while quietly aching for someone I could lean on in the same way. I've had many conversations in this past year about how losing people—whether to life or to death—can knock the wind out of you. Nikki's death forced me to face the fragility and urgency of life. It reminded me that tomorrow isn't promised, and that we have to live boldly and carry out our purpose now so the ripple of our calling continues even when we're gone. Legacy, legacy, legacy.

The gag is that breakthroughs rarely look or feel like blessings. They often arrive disguised as challenges—bills you can't pay, aches you can't shake, or losses you don't know how to navigate. They strip you down to the real you and force you to look in the mirror, humming Adele: *"Hello, it's me. I was wondering if after all these years you'd like to meet... They say that time's supposed to heal ya, but I ain't done much healing."*

It's in these moments that leadership stops being theory or a framework—it's a foundational element to my survival. For me, it means deliberately bringing all of who I am—my experiences, values, flaws, and faith—into how I show up. Because the real work doesn't happen in the spotlight. It happens in the silent, mostly dark moments when the duct tape is showing, my mascara is running, and my prayers feel unanswered.

Just in case you haven't caught on yet (I'm going to hold your hand when I say this) breakthrough isn't instant. It's incremental. It's akin to watering a seed every day without seeing a sprout. Honestly, that's what the last few years have felt like—me pouring into others while struggling to see my own growth. To me, that is a season of breakthrough. It's showing up when my cup feels empty, only to hear someone say, "You save lives," "You saved my life," or "You saved my career." It's moments like that when I remember that the ripple of our obedience travels further than we could ever imagine. To witness even a glimpse of the ripple...is a blessing.

Faith is not a filter. Faith is publicly walking the promises that were once whispered in private. Even when it hurts. Especially when it hurts.

The thing about breakthroughs is they don't just belong to us. When I come out on the other side of my breakdowns, whether it's in the hospital bed, Amazon Flex tears, or grief that nearly swallows me whole, I don't walk out empty-handed. I carry something forward. And the minute I share it, live it, or build from it, it creates a ripple. That's the part we don't always talk about. Your obedience isn't just for you. It's for everybody who's connected to you.

If you're in a season that feels like breakdown after breakdown, don't quit. Consider the flower. To bloom, it has to crack open, push through dirt, fight for light. We only admire the petals—we forget the breaking process. You, too, are in the soil of your next breakthrough. Hold on. The roots you're growing now will be the strength that carries you later. Just keep holding on.

ALL YOU GOTTA DO IS SAY YES

I've learned that my obedience doesn't just benefit me. My dad used to tell me, "You can't complain about something you aren't willing to do something about." That line lives rent-free in my head. It's probably the reason I couldn't just sit back and grumble about gaps I saw in leadership, publishing, or coaching. His words keep me accountable. If I see the problem, I know that I am also responsible for being part of the solution. That gap between knowing and doing is where leadership either grows or unravels.

That's exactly how *My Best SHIFT* came to life. Juneteenth was coming and the world seemed busy debating if it should be a holiday or not— while some Black people and African-Americans were admitting publicly that they didn't even know what it was. I was shocked. People older than me saying they had no clue? My inner voice was like, *What are they teaching in these school systems?!* In the middle of my rant, I felt God tapping me on the shoulder: *"Don't complain. Do something."*

So I called my now creative director, Janae, and floated the idea of recording a video explaining Juneteenth. She loved it—and then asked, "You mean tomorrow?" (HA! Bless her heart—she was a real one.) We stayed up all night recording and re-recording on a makeshift setup, me nervous as ever and taking a shot or two just to relax. Somewhere in that chaos, Janae looked at me and said, *"This is your shift. You're stepping out of the shadows and really shifting."*

… And boom! Just like that, with one act of obedience, My Best SHIFT was born, and the foundation for everything—CC Media, Conscious Leadership Collective, an award-winning podcast, bestselling books, summits, speaking engagements, coaching and more. Thousands impacted, not just by me, but by every author, every story, every listener. That's the ripple. And it keeps multiplying.

It's important to remember that ripples don't require perfection. They require movement. Think about throwing a stone in the water. The stone doesn't have to be smooth or flawless to make waves—it just has to move. That's what obedience looks like. It doesn't mean I have it all figured out. It means I'm willing to move, even when it's inconvenient, even when I don't feel ready.

I've seen this play out for others, too. One sister-friend said "yes" to creating the *Limitless Retreat*. Through her "yes"—or ripple, if you will—whole communities have been impacted, opportunities were birthed, and friendships have taken root. Another sister-friend who attended the *Limitless Retreat* hosts events that pour into people with so much intentionality, you can see the ripple effect unfold through connections formed, communities strengthened, lives changed.

That's the power of obedience: one yes sparks another, and before you know it, you've got a wave. And when those waves start to move, they don't just stir the water, they create moments, change lives, and call us back to purpose. Mark Twain once said, *"The two most important days in your life are the day you are born and the day you find out why."* I'd add a third: the day you have the courage to walk in your purpose. It's not always butterflies and rainbows, but it's worth every tear, "and sleepless night." Because obedience creates waves far beyond your line of sight. Legacy whispered, legacy witnessed, legacy lived. It's the footprint we leave, the ripple that keeps moving long after we are gone.

Obedience is contagious. Just like disobedience has consequences, obedience has dividends. When I say yes, it makes it easier for the next person to say yes. When I share my truth, it gives someone else permission to stop hiding. When I build, even in fear, it allows someone else to believe they can build too. The countless number of people who have said they started a podcast, created affirmation cards, journals, or wrote a book because they saw what I've been able to create is amazing. I'll never forget when a mentee told me how happy she was to see me wear color on my nails. Something that, for me, was an internal middle finger to "professionalism" was, for her, permission to show up as herself. That's the power of authenticity—it ripples too.

For me, obedience is about being in alignment. Making sure my actions line up with my values, my words, and my calling. Am I perfect? Absolutely not! However, I do know that disobedience has a ripple, too. It creates confusion and chaos. Pastor Sheryl Brady once said, *"My story is in my stones."* That resonates. Every step of obedience leaves evidence— not just for me, but for the people coming behind me. The stories I tell, the scars I share, the shifts I make—they're stones I lay down as proof that God met me there. And every time I put one down, it becomes a stone someone else can stand on, its impact sending ripples farther than I can see.

Every ripple traces back to its source. And that source is me. The work. The "yes." The courage to love myself enough to lead myself first. Because obedience isn't just about me. My "yes" is bigger than me. My authenticity is bigger than me. The ripples I set in motion might just be the waves that carry someone into or out of their breakthrough. Or, as Beyoncé put it best: "If you feel insignificant, you better think again… you're part of something way bigger."

AUDACIOUS ENOUGH TO BE REAL

Your purpose may be bigger than you, but it still begins with you. Loving yourself enough to honor your calling, to sit with your contradictions, to keep moving when it would be easier to stop—that's the real work. That's the love story I'm writing with myself every single day.

I've learned the hard way that I can't keep pouring from an empty cup. And yet, for years, I did just that—cheering for everyone else, showing up for everyone else, fighting for everyone else. Leading from within has taught me that the most radical shift isn't when I get on a stage or publish a book. It's when I choose myself. Not the polished, filtered me—the me with mascara smudged, edges frayed, voice trembling. Because if I can't lead her with kindness, honesty and love, then nothing else really matters.

Leading from within is what happens when vulnerability shakes hands with authenticity at the intersection of courage and truth. It's choosing courage over comfort and truth over performance. And that's how I lead—one yes, one stone, one ripple at a time. I'm still figuring it out, and I'm here. I'm choosing me, and that is enough. The question is: who or what will you choose?

If you take nothing else from my chapter, take this: you don't have to wait until you feel ready. You don't have to wait until you've "healed enough." You don't even have to wait until the duct tape is tucked out of sight.

Because whether you're leading a team, writing your first book, or just trying to find your way through transition, your story, your voice, and your presence matter. The world doesn't need the perfect version of you—it needs the real you. That's how we shift from just existing to truly being. And as you do, know this: you're not alone. Every courageous choice you make creates a ripple. Every act of authenticity is an invitation.

And suddenly—you show up. And suddenly—you choose yourself. And that, my friend, is how we shift—together.

ABOUT THE AUTHOR

CHANTÉE
L. CHRISTIAN

Chantée L. Christian is an ambassador of awareness with two decades of experience in management consulting and coaching. As founder of My Best SHIFT, she helps leaders align strategy with self-awareness to lead with intention, clarity, and authenticity.

She brings a unique blend of emotional intelligence, business acumen, and social impact to clients across sectors, including Fortune 500 companies, nonprofits, universities, and federal agencies. At the core of her work is a commitment to being a catalyst for growth and change through inspired action.

Chantée is the founder of CC Media, the publishing imprint behind the acclaimed bestseller *Awareness Put Me On*. A 3x bestselling author and award-winning podcaster, she also created Unspoken Truths of Being Black, an award-winning series that explores critical issues through the lens of heightened awareness and lived experience. In 2021, she was recognized as a Northern Virginia 40 Under 40 honoree for her cross-sector leadership and community impact.

A lifelong learner, Chantée holds a bachelor's degree from George Mason University and an MBA from Webster University. She is a Professional Certified Coach (PCC), a Myers-Briggs Type Indicator (MBTI) Certified Practitioner, a Certified Change Management Professional (CCMP), and holds a Strategic Diversity, Equity, and Inclusion Management Executive Certificate from Georgetown University.

Beyond the titles and accolades, she's a true Aquarius who moves to the beat of her own drum. She enjoys a good libation, traveling, and shopping (even if only through the window). Most of all, she loves belly laughs and creating core memories.

ACKNOWLEDGMENTS
From Chantée L. Christian, With Love!

Bringing this book to life was a transformative journey that lived up to its title in every way. The universe reminded me what *Leading From Within* truly takes—what it feels, looks, and even smells like. I leaned on many of the tools and practices shared in these chapters to stay the course so that we could create this incredible book. To say I'm proud would be an understatement.

I wouldn't have survived this journey without the support, encouragement, and love of so many people. For the sake of space, I can't name everyone. Please know if your name isn't listed here, it's not because I forgot you. I see you, I appreciate you, and I'm forever grateful for your role in my life.

To **Dyana Langley-Robinson**, thank you for planting the seed for this book series and NOT letting up on watering it and making sure it stayed top of mind for me. This project probably wouldn't have come to fruition without your not-so-subtle nudges. To **Samantha Armstrong**, you have been my right hand in this project. I don't know what I would've done without your guidance, our GIF exchanges, and daily reality checks. Thank you for sharing your gift with the world and your friendship with me. I appreciate you more than you will ever know.

A heartfelt thank you to our foreword author, **Angela R. McCullough**. From our first meeting at the *Limitless Retreat* to our time in Costa Rica shaping your book, these full-circle moments have shown me what it truly means to walk in purpose and be in community with excellence. Keep showing up as the fabulous force of nature that you are! The world needs you! To our book cover designer, **Ida Brown**, thank you for agreeing to yet another one of my *bright ideas*. I'm so grateful you're in my orbit, helping me bring to life something the world can adore and cherish just as much as I do.

To my **fellow authors** of *Leading From Within*, you all really did the damn thing! I asked you to be vulnerable, to lean into the parts of your story that other leaders might have kept tucked away or at a very surface level. You brought your truths, your courage, and your lived experiences to these pages, and in doing so gave others permission to see themselves. Thank you for your courage, honesty, and willingness to step into this vision with me. I'm forever grateful for your "YES" to amplifying your voices and showing the world what conscious leadership looks like in real life.

Even in the middle of my own storm of resistance and excuses, I knew I couldn't miss this moment to build a movement that fills a void in leadership and answers prayers I once whispered, privately. To do that, I had to call a cease-and-desist on my own internal BS. Faith, for me, has been publicly walking out the prayers I once kept private. That meant acknowledging the call God placed on my heart and trusting Him with it, just as He trusted me. It required full-body obedience—no more half-stepping—so we could bring you this extraordinary collection of lived experiences. For that, I give myself a **BIG** round of applause.

I'd be remiss not to honor the late **Nikki Walker**, a co-author in *Awareness Put Me On*, and a friend. She passed away just as this project was beginning, and her loss weighed heavily on my heart. It made me pause and reflect on legacy—on how we choose to spend the time we're given. Seeing the outpouring of love for Nikki and hearing how she touched so many lives reignited my fire to keep going. To me, that's the very essence of *Leading From Within*.

Lastly, and certainly not least, to our family, friends, and supporters, **THANK YOU** for believing in us and supporting our dreams. We hope this body of work meets you exactly where you are and continues to walk with you on your journey of conscious leadership and truly leading from within. Because when we lead from within, we don't just change ourselves, we change the world.

REFERENCES

Chapter 1: *The Quiet Power of Turning Inward* – Jennifer Pihlaja
1. Brené Brown, *Rising Strong* (Random House, 2015).
2. Naval Ravikant, quoted in Eric Jorgenson, *The Almanack of Naval Ravikant* (Magrathea Publishing, 2020).

Chapter 2: *I Don't Have Cancer and My Dog Isn't Dead* – Darci L. Graves
1. Sara Bareilles, "Brave," *The Blessed Unrest* (Epic Records, 2013).

Chapter 3: *Flow Over Force: Lighting Your Path Forward* – Marquise "Bogey" McCoy
1. Definition of fear adapted from Oxford English Dictionary, "fear, n.," OED Online, accessed July 10, 2025.
2. Patanjali, *The Yoga Sutras of Patanjali*, translated by Edwin F. Bryant (North Point Press, 2009).

Chapter 4: *The Beautiful Paradox of Purpose* – Dionne Galloway
1. Joseph Campbell, *The Power of Myth* (Anchor Books, 1991).
2. Georgetown University, "Strategic Diversity, Equity and Inclusion Management Executive Certificate Program," accessed July 10, 2025.

Chapter 5: *Thoughtful Leadership: From the Ashes to Alignment* – Jacquelyn Bsharah, PhD
1. Maya Angelou, quoted in Wouldn't *Take Nothing for My Journey Now* (Random House, 1993).

Chapter 6: *The Gift of Disruption: Redirection and Joy* – Minetta Minor
2. American Psychological Association, "Post-Traumatic Growth: Finding Meaning in Adversity," *Monitor on Psychology*, 2019.
3. Proverbs 3:5–6 (New International Version).

Chapter 7: *There's a Rhythm, Measured Power* – Carl Mosby III
1. Jay-Z, "A Dream," Blueprint 2: *The Gift & The Curse* (Roc-A-Fella

Records, 2002).

2. Rakim, "Follow the Leader," *Follow the Leader* (MCA Records, 1988).

Chapter 8: *From Performance to Presence* – Ashley B. Stewart

1. Benjamin Elijah Mays, *Disturbed About Man* (Howard University Press, 1969).

2. bell hooks, *The Will to Change: Men, Masculinity, and Love* (Atria Books, 2004).

Chapter 9: *Rough Truths & Smooth R&B* – Dyana Langley-Robinson

1. Mary J. Blige, "Not Gon' Cry," *Waiting to Exhale Soundtrack* (Arista Records, 1995).

2. Monica, "Don't Take It Personal (Just One of Dem Days)," *Miss Thang* (Rowdy Records, 1995).

3. Luther Vandross, "A House Is Not a Home," *Never Too Much* (Epic Records, 1981).

4. Tevin Campbell, "Can We Talk," *I'm Ready* (Qwest/Warner Bros., 1993).

5. Maxwell, "Ascension (Don't Ever Wonder)," Maxwell's *Urban Hang Suite* (Columbia Records, 1996).

6. Troop, "All I Do Is Think of You," *Attitude* (Atlantic Records, 1989).

7. Diana Ross, "I'm Coming Out," *diana* (Motown Records, 1980).

8. For further details regarding my history of truancy, see my chapter "50 Shades of Gray" in *Awareness Put Me On*, ed. Chantée Christian (CC Media, 2024), pg. 227–238.

Chapter 10: *To Play or Not to Play the Game* – Dominique Hollins

1. Elizabeth Magie, *The Landlord's Game*, patented 1904.

2. Rumi, quoted in Coleman Barks, *The Essential Rumi* (HarperOne, 1995).

3. Harvard Business Review, "Why Diversity Programs Fail," https://hbr.org/2016/07/why-diversity-programs-fail, accessed July 10, 2025.

Chapter 11: *From Legacy to Leadership: Lessons My Father Never Spoke but Always Lived* – James Harris

1. Langston Hughes, "Live Your Creed," in *The Collected Poems of Langston Hughes* (Vintage Classics, 1995).
2. Proverbs 22:6 (New King James Version).

Chapter 12: *And Suddenly…Shift Happens* – Chantée L. Christian
1. Brené Brown, Daring Greatly: How the Courage to Be Vulnerable Transforms the Way We Live, Love, Parent, and Lead (New York: Gotham Books, 2012).
2. Alicia Keys, "Superwoman," track 14 on *As I Am*, J Records, 2007, CD.
3. Shawn "Jay-Z" Carter, "Public Service Announcement (Interlude)," track 8 on The Black Album, Roc-A-Fella Records, 2003, CD.
4. Chantée L. Christian, "Ceasing and Desisting The Internal B.S.," in *Awareness Put Me On* (Virginia: CC Media Productions, 2023).
5. Erykah Badu, "Tyrone," track 7 on Live, Universal Records, 1997, CD.
6. Lauryn Hill, "Nothing Even Matters," track 14 on T*he Miseducation of Lauryn Hill*, Ruffhouse/Columbia Records, 1998, CD.
7. Leonard Cohen, "Anthem," track 5 on The *Future*, Columbia Records, 1992, CD.
8. Rumi, adapted from Coleman Barks, *The Essential Rumi* (San Francisco: HarperSanFrancisco, 1995).
9. Paul Engemann, "Push It to the Limit," in *Scarface: Music from the Original Motion Picture Soundtrack*, MCA Records, 1983, vinyl.
10. "The Golden Girls," created by Susan Harris, featuring Estelle Getty as Sophia Petrillo, NBC, 1985–1992.
11. Anthony Hamilton, "I'm a Mess," track 9 on *Comin' from Where I'm From*, So So Def/Arista, 2003, CD.
12. Tasha Cobbs Leonard, "Gracefully Broken," track 10 on *Heart. Passion. Pursuit.*, Motown Gospel, 2017, CD.
13. Shawn "Jay-Z" Carter, *4:44*, Roc Nation Records, 2017, digital.
14. Adele, "Hello," track 1 on 25, XL/Columbia Records, 2015, CD.
15. Floetry, "Say Yes," track 11 on *Floetic*, DreamWorks Records, 2002, CD.
16. Beyoncé, "Bigger," track 1 on *The Lion King: The Gift,* Parkwood Entertainment/Columbia Records, 2019, digital.

ABOUT
LEADING FROM WITHIN

Leading From Within is the first volume of the Conscious Leadership Collective, a groundbreaking anthology published by CC Media. Featuring thirteen bold voices—executives, entrepreneurs, coaches, and creatives—this book redefines leadership by centering authenticity, lived experience, and conscious choice.

Far more than a collection of essays, *Leading From Within* is a movement: amplifying underrepresented voices, disrupting outdated leadership paradigms, and using story as a catalyst for healing and transformation. Each chapter is handcrafted through coaching, reflection, and collaboration to model conscious leadership in action.

With nearly 40 authors supported through CC Media's publishing and coaching, this work reflects our core values of authenticity, integrity, representation, transformation, and courage. Leading From Within isn't just a book—it's a call to lead with truth, vulnerability, and boldness from the inside out.

THE SOUNDTRACK OF
LEADING FROM WITHIN

Curated by the authors of *Leading From Within*, this playlist mirrors the chapters themselves—woven with resilience, healing, vulnerability, authenticity, and truth. Every chapter, every song, holds the rhythm of resilience, the honesty of vulnerability, and the beauty of truth.

SCAN TO LISTEN ON SPOTIFY

FEATURING SONGS LIKE: "BIGGER" • "BRAVE" • "LEGACY"